# SEALS + PLUS

## reproducible activity-based handouts
## created for teachers & counselors

(Adapted from **Life Management Skills I** and **II**)

## A sampler collection of. . .

| | | |
|---|---|---|
| Anger Management | Goal Setting | Self-Esteem/Awareness |
| Assertion | Health Awareness | Stress Management |
| Communication Skills | Money Management | Support Systems |
| Coping Skills | Problem Solving | Time Management |
| Emotion Identification | Risk Taking | Values Clarification |

**Authors:** Kathy L. Korb, OTR/L, Stacey D. Azok, OTR/L, Estelle A. Leutenberg, Graphic Artist
**Adapted By:** Elaine M. Hyla, M.Ed.
**Illustrated By:** Amy L. Leutenberg, BA, BFA

WELLNESS
REPRODUCTIONS
INCORPORATED

# THANK YOU!

**SEALS+PLUS IS DEDICATED TO ERWIN LEFFEL . . .**

who inspired the development of the original SEALS program, and who made it possible for us to see that program evolve into this SEALS+PLUS publication. We thank you, Erwin, for your encouragement, support, and belief in the value of self-esteem and life skill programming in the schools.

**THANK YOU TO ELAINE HYLA . . .**

who used her expertise as an educator, and her experience with the SEALS program, to adapt LIFE MANAGEMENT SKILLS I & II for this school-based SEALS+PLUS publication. Elaine M. Hyla, M. Ed., graduated from Kent State University in 1973, majoring in Secondary Education, and from Cleveland State University in 1987, earning an M.Ed. in Curriculum and Instruction, specializing in Emerging Adolescence. She is presently a middle school librarian. Her work with adolescents has earned for her, inclusion in Who's Who in American Education, 1989-90. Elaine is completing a second master's degree in Library Science at Kent State University.

**THANK YOU TO AMY LEUTENBERG . . .**

our Wellness Reproductions artist, whose creativity and skill as an illustrator, and experience with adolescents, gave the SEALS+PLUS book unique, humorous, and meaningful artwork. Amy L. Leutenberg graduated from Kent State University with a B.A. in Art Education and a B.F.A. in Studio Art. She continues to pursue her career as an artist, and is in her senior year in the Master's Program at the Mandel School of Applied Social Sciences at Case Western Reserve University. For the past two years Amy has been facilitating wellness with at-risk children and their families.

**THANK YOU TO DONNA URBAN . . .**

our Wellness Reproductions office administrator, for her valued input, honest feedback and ongoing dedication. We admire and appreciate her commitment and sincere investment in our company and in the Wellness philosophy.

**THANK YOU TO THE WILLOWICK MIDDLE SCHOOL CORE TEAM . . .**

for their support, feedback, and encouragement.

# INTRODUCTION

The inspiration for the LIFE MANAGEMENT SKILLS SERIES originated from an ongoing practical need observed within a mental health setting. Handouts had been typically used in treatment as a launching pad for activities, an organizational tool, a visual aid, a tangible reminder of information presented, and as a method for building rapport. However, available handouts often did not meet necessary, high-quality standards in content desired, format, appearance, and organization - and lacked copyright permission for reproduction.

We have attempted to meet these standards by offering this collection of handouts which are highly reproducible, organized in 15 logical units, designed for specific well-defined purposes, and activity-based, allowing for extensive student involvement. The graphic representations are intentionally different from handout to handout in typestyle, art, and design, to increase visual appeal, provide variety, clarify meaning, and initiate and stimulate class discussions.

SEALS+PLUS is a selection of activity handouts from the original LIFE MANAGEMENT SKILLS books I & II. They have been adapted for use with middle school through high school-aged students. Illustrations, verbiage and content have been focused to meet the concerns and needs of this population.

The book has been designed to offer reproducible handouts on the front of each page and nonreproducible facilitator's information on the reverse side. The Teacher/Facilitator's Information Sheet (reverse of each handout) includes the following sections: Purpose, General Comments, and Possible Activities; Activity A designed for the middle school student, Activity B for the high school student.

A TEACHER'S BONUS SECTION has been included to help facilitators utilize SEALS+PLUS, and can offer assistance if SEALS+PLUS is to be implemented as a program. We hope you find these pages to be time-saving and beneficial.

We specifically chose spiral binding to allow for easier and accurate reproduction, an especially white paper for clear, sharp copies, and a heavier paper stock for its durability and opacity. If adaptations to any of the handouts are desired, it is recommended to make one copy of the handout, include the changes which will meet your specific needs, and then use this copy as the original.

We hope you find these handouts fun, innovative, and informative. Try to incorporate students' input in planning and presenting SEALS+PLUS sessions, to promote variety, facilitate learning, and individualize sessions. We wish you much success with your educational endeavors and hope we can be of assistance again in the future. Remember...creative handouts will hopefully generate creative activities and contribute to a greater sense of WELLNESS!

*Kathy L. Korb*          *Stacey D. Azok*          *Estelle A. Leutenberg*

# WELLNESS REPRODUCTIONS INCORPORATED

**WELLNESS REPRODUCTIONS INC.** is an innovative company which began in 1988, by Kathy L. Korb, OTR/L, Stacey D. Azok, OTR/L, and Estelle A. Leutenberg. As developers of creative therapeutic and educational products and services, we have a strong commitment to the development of self-esteem and life skills. Our rapidly growing business began by authoring and self-publishing the book LIFE MANAGEMENT SKILLS. We have extended our product line to include LIFE MANAGEMENT SKILLS II, group presentation posters, the EMOTIONS products, the BRIDGE OF SELF-CONFIDENCE board game, the school-based SEALS program (Self-Esteem and Life Skills), an annual NET•WORK•SHOP, a videotape regarding serious mental illness, and now, another book, SEALS+PLUS. This book was created with feedback from our customers and adapted for middle school through high school from LIFE MANAGEMENT SKILLS I and II. Please refer to the last page of this book, our "FEEDBACK" page, and let us hear from YOU!

23945 Mercantile Road • Beachwood, Ohio 44122-5924
800/669-9208 • FAX 216/831-1355

# TABLE OF CONTENTS

# TABLE OF CONTENTS

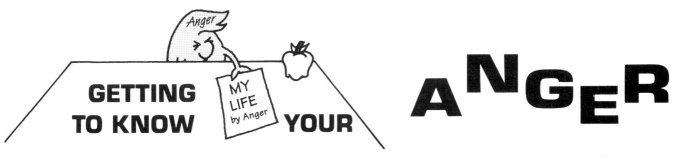

# GETTING TO KNOW YOUR ANGER

MY LIFE by Anger

Anger is a normal, human emotion. It is intense. Everyone gets angry and has a right to his/her anger. The trick is managing your anger effectively so that it will move you in POSITIVE, not negative, directions.

The first step in **ANGER MANAGEMENT** is to get to know your anger by recognizing its symptoms.

## DO YOU . . .

| physical | emotional | behavioral |
|---|---|---|
| __ grit your teeth? | __ feel like running away? | __ cry/yell/scream? |
| __ get a headache? | __ get depressed? | __ use substances? |
| __ get sweaty palms? | __ feel guilty? | __ get sarcastic? |
| __ get dizzy? | __ feel resentment? | __ lose sense of humor? |
| __ get red-faced? | __ become anxious? | __ become abusive? |
| __ get a stomachache? | __ feel like lashing out? | __ withdraw? |
| __ _____ | __ _____ | __ _____ |
| __ _____ | __ _____ | __ _____ |

## DOES YOUR ANGER . . .

__ last too long?                                   __ make you feel ill?
__ become too intense?                         __ come too frequently?
__ lead to aggression?                           __ flare up too quickly?
__ hurt relationships?                            __ _____
__ prevent you from doing your work at home or at school?   __ _____
__ creep out in mysterious ways?           __ _____

## ANGER INVENTORY (Rate 1-5) Rank your anger in the following situations.

| 1 - no annoyance | 2 - little irritated | 3 - upset | 4 - quite angry | 5 - very angry |
|---|---|---|---|---|

__ You've overheard people joking about you, your family, or your friends.
__ You're not being treated with respect or consideration.
__ You're singled out for corrections while the actions of others go unnoticed.
__ You're hounded by a salesperson from the moment you walk into a store.
__ You're trying to discuss something important with someone, who isn't giving you a chance to talk or express your feelings.
__ Someone offers continual, unsolicited advice.
__ You're in a discussion with someone who persists in arguing about a topic s/he knows very little about.
__ You've had a busy day and your parents/guardians greet you with complaints about what you haven't finished.
__ Someone is given special consideration because of his/her popularity, good looks, financial position, or family status.
__ Someone comments on your being overweight/underweight.
__ **TOTAL**

Additional situations that spark YOUR anger.

_____

_____

_____

## ...perhaps it's time to work on your anger management skills!

 **ANGER**

I. PURPOSE:

To increase knowledge and awareness of physical, behavioral and emotional anger symptoms.

II. GENERAL COMMENTS:

Oftentimes, anger is misunderstood and unrecognized. Getting to know your anger and confronting it is the first step in effective anger management.

III. POSSIBLE ACTIVITIES: Discuss all new or challenging vocabulary.

A. 1. Distribute handouts and review. When discussing "anger inventory", remind students that mismanaged anger will have a negative effect on physical and emotional health.

2. Ask students to share their totals. Record the frequency of the totals. Ask students to explain the meaning of the anger inventory totals, e.g., "What do the anger inventory totals tell about the way anger is managed if most of (part of) (some of) the class scored in the 45-50 range, 40-44, etc. range?"

3. Instruct students to write anger vertically 3 times on the back of each handout.

| A | A | A |
| N | N | N |
| G | G | G |
| E | E | E |
| R | R | R |

4. Ask students to use the first set of letters to describe their physical anger symptoms in words or phrases, e.g.,

        A - aches
        N - nausea
        G - gritting teeth
        E - energy loss
        R - rigid posture

5. Continue using the second set for emotional anger symptoms.

6. Finish with the third set for behavioral anger symptoms.

7. Encourage sharing of students' responses by listing them on the chalkboard.

8. Process benefits of increased awareness of personal anger symptoms.

B. 1. Distribute handouts and review. When discussing "anger inventory", ask students to share their totals. Remind them that unmanaged anger will have a negative effect on physical and mental health.

2. Complete handouts.

3. If class expresses a desire for an interpretation of the "anger inventory", see Activity A, Section 2 for procedure.

4. Direct class into pairs for sharing of responses. Allot time for both partners to share in detail (approximately 15-20 minutes).

5. Reconvene the class and give each group member 1-2 minutes to summarize his/her partner's anger profile. Encourage feedback from others as appropriate.

6. Process benefits of this activity.

☑ STUFFING — a passive style of coping with anger.
— not allowing yourself to express anger in an open way.

## Do you "stuff" your anger? _____

## Do you tend to avoid open, honest and direct communication about why you are angry?_____

*"Stuffers" can deny anger...*

*they may not admit to themselves or to others that they are angry.*

*"Stuffers" may not be aware that they have the <u>right</u> to be angry.*

Some reasons we "stuff" are:

1] fear of hurting/offending someone. ☐

2] fear of being disliked or rejected. ☐

3] fear of losing control. ☐

4] feeling it's inappropriate (not ok) to be angry. ☐

5] feeling unable to cope with such a strong, intense emotion. ☐

6] fear of damaging/losing a relationship. ☐

7] it's a learned behavior (but, it can be unlearned!). ☐

8] _____

9] _____

10] _____

Results/Outcome:

1] anger comes out — regardless.

2] hurts relationships.

3] affects physical and mental health.

4] _____

5] _____

WELCOME!

I. PURPOSE:

To increase knowledge of the anger style called "stuffing".

To identify personal anger styles.

II. GENERAL COMMENTS:

"Stuffing" describes the passive style of coping with anger. Being able to identify a personal anger style is an early step in anger management.

III. POSSIBLE ACTIVITIES: This handout can be used in conjunction with GETTING TO KNOW YOUR ANGER (page 1),
ANGER STYLES - ESCALATING     (page 3),
ANGER STYLES - MANAGING I      (page 4), and
ANGER STYLES - MANAGING II     (page 5).

A. 1. Distribute handouts.

2. Discuss the definition of stuffing, encouraging students to offer comments and descriptions of a person who might "stuff" anger.

3. Attempt to list T.V./movie/book/cartoon characters, historical figures and occupations that demonstrate the "stuffing" style.

4. If time permits, introduce ANGER STYLES - ESCALATING page as the next step in this Anger Awareness and Anger Management Module.

5. If time permits, introduce ANGER STYLES - MANAGING I & II pages as a more effective style of anger management.

6. Lead discussion and process problems and potential implications associated with the "stuffing" style and the benefits of managing.

B. 1. Discuss the topic of "stuffing" briefly.

2. Encourage each student to share a situation in which s/he "stuffed" anger, why, and consequences resulting.

3. Distribute handouts and complete as a class activity, recalling prior discussion. Recall examples as listed in Anger Inventory (page 1) to aid discussion.

4. Discuss benefits of greater self-awareness and ask each student to set a short-term goal to learn effective anger management skills.

# ANGER STYLES

☐ STUFFING     ☑ ESCALATING     ☐ MANAGING

☑ ESCALATING — an aggressive style of coping with anger.
— a heated, extreme reaction to a situation.

## Do you "escalate" to rage? _____

## Do you try to control, but lose control? _____

*"Escalators" blame and shame the "provoker".*

*"Escalating" often leads to hurtful situations.*

Some reasons we escalate are:

1] feeling "I have no other choice". ☐

2] to demonstrate an image of strength/power. ☐

3] to avoid expressing underlying emotions. ☐

4] fear of getting close to someone. ☐

5] it's the only response we have been taught. ☐

6] lack of communication skills. ☐

7] _____

8] _____

Results/Outcome:

1] desired results may be short-term.

2] possible physical destruction.

3] hurts relationships.

4] affects physical and mental health.

5] may cause legal problems.

6] _____

7] _____

I. PURPOSE:

To increase knowledge of the anger style called "escalating".

To identify personal anger styles.

II. GENERAL COMMENTS:

"Escalating" describes the aggressive style of coping with anger. Being able to identify a personal anger style is an early step in anger management.

III. POSSIBLE ACTIVITIES: This handout can be used in conjunction with ANGER STYLES - STUFFING      (page 2),
    ANGER STYLES - MANAGING I  (page 4), and
    ANGER STYLES - MANAGING II  (page 5).

A.  1. Distribute handouts. Discuss new or challenging vocabulary.

2. Use illustration to aid discussion of the term "escalating". What does an escalator do? Why are the two characters riding on the escalator? Where is the escalator taking them? Complete the page, using the students' examples.

3. Attempt to list T.V./movie/book/cartoon characters, historical figures, and occupations that demonstrate the "escalating" style.

4. Discuss, encouraging students to offer comments regarding this anger style.

5. Review the ANGER-STYLES - STUFFING page.

6. If time permits, introduce ANGER STYLES - MANAGING I & II pages as a more effective style of anger management.

7. Process problems associated with the "escalating" style and benefits of managing.

B.  1. Review topic of "escalating" briefly.

2. Encourage students to share a situation in which s/he "escalated" to rage, why, and resulting consequences.

3. Distribute handouts and complete as a class activity, recalling prior discussion about ANGER-STUFFING.

4. Discuss benefits of greater self-awareness and ask each student to set a short-term goal to learn effective anger management skills.

☑ MANAGING — an assertive style of coping with anger situations.
— the most effective style of coping with anger situations.

*I'm really working hard on managing my anger — so . . . I need to talk to you. I feel angry when . . .*

## Do you "manage" your anger?_____

## Do you allow anger to move you in positive directions? _____

*OPEN, HONEST AND DIRECT EXPRESSION is the most effective way of managing anger.*
*Easier said than done, huh? When expressing anger directly, keep these important skills in mind...*

• Remind yourself that anger is a normal, human emotion...
   it's OK to feel angry! Give yourself permission to feel anger.
• Before *open, honest and direct expression*, consider the following:
   What was the event that triggered your anger?      Is this good timing for the listener?
• Set a specific time limit for anger discussion.
• Be aware of the power of your body language:
   firm voice — moderate tone — direct eye contact —
   maintain personal "space" —establish an even eye-level with the listener.
• Avoid attacking or blaming.
• Focus on the specific behavior that triggered your anger.
• Avoid *black and white* thinking.
   "You never _____," INSTEAD, try "I'd prefer that _____, then I would feel _____."
• Use "I" statements.
   "I" feel angry when . . . "
• Avoid statements/actions that you'll regret later.
• This is not the time to drag in old, unresolved issues.
• Check for possible compromises.
• After *open, honest and direct* discussion, close the discussion, and move on.
• When it's over, pat yourself on the back for your assertiveness!
• Say to yourself "I (and perhaps the people around me) will be better off in the long run!"

**NOW say to yourself —**
   **"By managing my anger, I took an important step in improving my sense of well-being!"**

I.  PURPOSE:

To increase knowledge of the anger style called "managing".

To identify personal anger styles.

II.  GENERAL COMMENTS:

Managing anger is the most effective method in coping with anger situations. Managing anger by *open, honest and direct expression* is the most effective, yet challenging method. For many, this assertive approach takes effort, energy, time and practice.

III. POSSIBLE ACTIVITIES: This handout can be used in conjunction
with ANGER STYLES - STUFFING     (page 2),
     ANGER STYLES - ESCALATING (page 3), and
     ANGER STYLES - MANAGING II (page 5).

A.  1.  Distribute handouts following discussion of "stuffing" and "escalating".

2.  Discuss all new and challenging vocabulary.

3.  Discuss handout.

4.  Prepare slips of paper. Give each student one slip of paper. Instruct students to describe, in writing, a situation in which they have been angry. Collect the slips and place them in a hat.

5.  Each student then chooses one slip from the hat and proceeds to role-play the situation showing <u>mismanaged</u> anger. Discuss the role-play.

6.  Instruct the students to re-create the role-play. This time, instruct the students to follow suggestions for <u>effective anger management</u> which were discussed on the handout.

7.  Process benefits of open, honest and direct expression of anger.

B.  1.  Distribute handouts following discussion of "stuffing" and "escalating".

2.  Discuss all new and challenging vocabulary.

3.  Provide discussion, explanation, demonstration, role-plays, etc. of this anger management technique that would benefit the specific age or grade level.

4.  Process benefits of open, honest and direct expression of anger.

# ANG▢R STYL▢S

▢ STUFFING     ▢ ESCALATING     ☑ MANAGING II

☑ MANAGING — an assertive style of coping with anger situations.
      — the most effective style of coping with anger situations.

## Do you "manage" your anger?_____
## Do you allow anger to mobilize you in positive directions?_____

*OPEN, HONEST AND DIRECT EXPRESSION*
*is the most effective way of managing anger.*
*[ see Anger Styles - Managing I ]*

STUFFING

ESCALATING

MANAGING

Increases daily energy level

Develops effective communication skills

Strengthens relationships

Improves physical and mental health

Boosts self-esteem

*Other effective anger management techniques are:*

1] Choosing constructive (not destructive) methods / solutions / ideas.

2] Involving an impartial third party.

3] Using the "empty chair" exercise.

4] Writing a letter.

5] Using relaxation techniques.

6] Using positive self-talk.

7] Working towards anger resolution through acceptance.

8] List other anger management techniques:

_____

_____

_____

## *REMEMBER — anger is a normal human emotion.*

I.  PURPOSE:
To increase knowledge of the anger style called "managing".
To identify personal anger styles.

II.  GENERAL COMMENTS:
Managing anger is the most effective method in coping with anger situations. This assertive approach offers many effective techniques.

III.  POSSIBLE ACTIVITIES: This handout can be used in conjunction
with ANGER STYLES - STUFFING      (page 2),
    ANGER STYLES - ESCALATING (page 3), and/or
    ANGER STYLES - MANAGING I (page 4).

A.  1.  Distribute handouts. Discuss all new or challenging vocabulary.
   2.  Prepare enough slips of paper so that each student receives three slips.
   3.  Instruct all students to write three anger-provoking situations each on separate pieces of paper and place in a hat.
   4.  Divide class into small groups and instruct each group to choose three situations from the hat. Provide them with three sheets of paper.
   5.  Instruct each small group of students to identify two effective "management" techniques from the handout that would help with each of the anger situations chosen from the hat. Allow 15-20 minutes to complete either a written summary of their ideas or instruct them to illustrate and color a picture of each of their three summaries. (If unable to provide colored pencils, crayons or markers for each group, remind class to bring in their own.)
   6.  Return to class and have a representative from each small group share their summary.
   7.  Process benefits of the "management" style.
   8.  Time permitting, ask for two volunteers to select one situation from the remaining slips and role-play a response to the anger-provoking situation. The role-play must demonstrate the "management" techniques discussed on the handout.

B.  1.  Distribute handouts. Discuss all new or challenging vocabulary.
   2.  Provide discussion, explanation, demonstration, role-plays, etc. of the anger management techniques that would benefit the specific age group or grade level.
   3.  Process benefits of the "management" style.
   4.  The following outline can be used to supplement discussions of anger management techniques.
      1.]  Choosing constructive (not destructive) methods/solutions/ideas.
         a.)  Trying physical outlets, e.g., exercise, housework, crafts, etc.
         b.)  Problem solving and coming up with action plans, e.g., forming a neighborhood recycling committee, organizing a garage sale, volunteering at a local senior citizens center, etc.
      2.]  Involving an impartial third party.
         a.)  Ask someone you trust to be a sounding board.
         b.)  Who might this be?
      3.]  Using the "empty chair" exercise.
         a.)  Pretend you're sitting across from the person you're angry with and say what's on your mind.
         b.)  Who is that person?
      4.]  Writing a letter to the person with whom you are angry.
         a.)  You could describe your anger right now, at the time of the anger situation or both.
         b.)  You can destroy the letter.
         c.)  You can save it.
         d.)  You can mail it at a later date.
      5.]  Using relaxation techniques.
         a.)  Self-help tapes.
         b.)  Music.
         c.)  Deep breathing.
      6.]  Using positive self-talk.
         a.)  "I am able to choose my anger style."
         b.)  "It's OK to be angry and I'm not going to let it…"
      7.]  Working toward anger resolution through acceptance.
         a.)  Learning to live with the fact that certain people, and situations past, present and future, may not change.
         b.)  Suggestions for learning acceptance:
            aa.)  Recall a frustrating anger situation.
            bb.)  Can you make this situation change as you would like it to?
            cc.)  If not, then practice:
               1.)  Making realistic expectations.
               2.)  Realizing the powerlessness over the situation.
               3.)  Giving yourself a time limit to be angry and then…let it go!
               4.)  Constantly reminding yourself "I cannot afford to stay angry. What's at stake here?"
               5.)  Recognize the need for forgiveness by saying: "No painful event is allowed to contribute to my anger more than one time."
               6.)  Focus on the present.

# ANGER DIARY

| DATE & TIME | |
|---|---|
| **FIRST SYMPTOM(S):** | |
| **WHAT TRIGGERED YOUR ANGER RESPONSE?** | |
| **YOUR RESPONSE:** | |
| **+ / −** <br> **GENERALLY, DO YOU THINK YOU DID WELL OR NOT SO WELL?** | |
| **WHAT WAS SOMETHING YOU DID WELL IN THIS SITUATION?** | |
| **IS THERE SOMETHING YOU CAN DO IN THE FUTURE TO BETTER MANAGE YOUR ANGER? WHAT?** | |

# ANGER DIARY

## I. PURPOSE:

To increase anger management skills by observing, recording and evaluating key events surrounding anger situations.

## II. GENERAL COMMENTS:

Anger situations often happen quickly, preventing accurate assessments of details and possible patterns. Diaries assist in the assessment process by allowing the individual to recall key events (some of which may be unpleasant), to record them in a logical, organized way, and later to evaluate them.

## III. POSSIBLE ACTIVITIES:

A. 1. Distribute handouts. Discuss any new or challenging vocabulary.

2. Provide a discussion of a diary. What is it? Why do people keep diaries? Name a famous diary, e.g., Anne Frank: Diary of a Young Girl, Go Ask Alice, Jay's Journal.

3. Provide an overview of an anger diary.

4. Prepare enough strips of paper so that each student receives three strips.

5. Instruct the class to write one anger-provoking situation on each. Collect all the strips and put them in a basket. To save time, recycle the papers or the illustrations from the previous activity (See ANGER STYLES-MANAGEMENT II page 5).

6. Ask each student to read aloud the situation and offer possible symptoms associated with it (See GETTING TO KNOW YOUR ANGER page 1), possible responses (positive and negative), specific things done well, and which could be managed better in the future.

7. Encourage students to identify which situations they have written and personal insights gained from class activity.

8. Encourage ongoing use of diary to monitor anger management skills and periodic discussion of diary with others for feedback.

9. Instruct class to bring a notebook or photocopy and staple together enough sheets of the ANGER DIARY so that each student has enough sheets for a week.

10. Schedule at least five minutes daily so that students can write entries in their diaries. Collect them daily. Assign one student to distribute them to the class daily at the assigned time. Assure them of the confidentiality of their entries. Offer this as an ongoing classroom activity.

B. 1. Provide handouts. Discuss all new and challenging vocabulary.

2. Provide brief description of the purposes of diaries.

3. Elicit examples of anger situations from students and record them on the chalkboard or overhead projector.

4. Using the ANGER DIARY page, make a transparency master, or copy the page by hand on a blank transparency. Use a permanent marker to create the transparency.

5. Choose one situation from the students' examples, proceed to complete the ANGER DIARY on the transparency using a washable overhead projector pen.

6. Process benefits of using a diary to increase anger management skills.

7. Follow-up by instructing students to purchase their own personal diaries or notebooks. For classroom activity, photocopy and staple together enough copies of the ANGER DIARY so that each student has enough copies for a week.

8. Schedule enough classtime daily so that students can write entries in their diaries. Collect them and assure the class of the confidentiality of this activity.

# Passive      Assertive      Aggressive

*Meet*
## Augusta Aggressive

I'm loud, bossy and pushy.
I dominate and intimidate people.
I violate other's rights.
I "get my way" at anyone's expense.
I "step" on people.
I react instantly.

*Meet*
## Abby Assertive

I'm firm, direct and honest.
I respect the rights of others and recognize the
importance of having my needs and rights
respected. I speak clearly and to the point.
I'm confident about who I am.
I realize I have choices about my life.

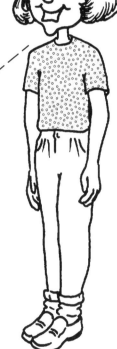

*Meet*
## Patsy Passive

I'm unable to speak up for my rights.
(I don't even know what my rights are!)
I get "stepped on" often.
I'm meek, mild-mannered and very accommodating.

# Female – Assertive

I. PURPOSE:

To recognize these three types of communication styles.

To increase awareness of the advantages of being assertive.

To recognize how these styles present themselves in females.

II. GENERAL COMMENTS:

This is an overview of the three basic communication styles, including nonverbal communication, view of rights, and implications of these behaviors. Communication is most effective when assertive.

III. POSSIBLE ACTIVITIES:

A. 1. Discuss all new or challenging vocabulary.

   2. Pursue a discussion of the names chosen to represent each communication style. Use an unabridged dictionary to research the meaning of the names and to find further clarification of the three communication styles, if needed. Discuss the characters' mode of dress, hairstyles, posture. Discuss the differences in the typeface chosen for each character's name and why that style was chosen.

   3. Instruct the class to list TV/cartoon/fictional/historical characters that resemble each communication style.

   4. Pursue a discussion of the potentially socialized role of females to be passive from childhood to adulthood, and the consequences. Discussion should include toys, clothing, sports, games and activities that females are encouraged and expected to play with or participate in. Discuss lyrics of popular songs and videos and the depiction of females in them. Discuss the differences between females and males in regards to academic expectations, rules for conduct and behavior, preferential treatment and disciplinary consequences.

B. 1. This activity is to be used in conjunction with Male—Assertive, page 8, when both females and males are in the class. Divide the class into two teams. Avoid segregating the groups by gender.

   2. Prepare several slips of paper with different situations and a different communication style, e.g.,
      Asking teacher for help with a difficult problem. ASSERTIVE
      Asking boss for a raise or promotion. PASSIVE

   3. Instruct a volunteer from Team #1 to select one slip and to role-play the situation listed on his/her paper. Within a specified time limit, Team #2 is to guess which style was being presented.

   4. The teams can repeat the process with Team #2 role-playing and Team #1 guessing.

   5. Continue alternating.

   6. Process group and review the differences in communication styles.

# Passive    # Assertive    # Aggressive

# Male – Assertive

## I. PURPOSE:

To recognize these three types of communication styles.

To increase awareness of the advantages of being assertive.

To recognize how these styles present themselves in males.

## II. GENERAL COMMENTS:

This is an overview of the three basic communication styles, including nonverbal communication, view of rights, and implications of these behaviors. Communication is most effective when assertive.

## III. POSSIBLE ACTIVITIES:

A. 1. Discuss all new or challenging vocabulary. Discuss the significance of the names chosen to represent each communication style. Use an unabridged dictionary to find the meaning of the names and to find further clarification of the three communication styles if needed. Discuss the characters' mode of dress, hairstyle, posture. Instruct the class to discuss the significance of the typestyle used for each character's speech.

2. Instruct the class to list TV/cartoon/fictional/historical characters that resemble each communication style.

3. Pursue a discussion of the socialized role of males to be aggressive from childhood through adulthood, and the consequences. Discussion could include toys, clothing, sports, games and activities that males are encouraged and expected to play with or participate in. Discuss the differences between females and males in regards to academic expectations, rules for behavior, preferential treatment and disciplinary consequences.

B. 1. This activity is designed to be used in conjunction with Female-Assertive, page 7, when both females and males are in the class. Facilitate role-playing of the three communication styles using the following examples:

a. A friend needs to borrow lunch money.

b. You want a raise in allowance.

c. Your boyfriend/girlfriend has not been paying enough attention to you.

d. You're in a restaurant and no one is waiting on you.

e. Any other situation considered to be relevant to the class age and/or grade level.

2. Process class and review the differences in communications styles.

# DON'T FALL IN THE TRAP.....
# ASK — DON'T ASSUME!

You have the **right** to ask questions!!

EVEN KIDS HAVE THE ABILITY AND OPPORTUNITIES TO BE

# ASSERTIVE!

| SITUATION | YOUR ASSUMPTION | YOU ASK | POSSIBLE RESPONSE(S) |
|---|---|---|---|
| *Friends were supposed to meet you at 6 o'clock but they arrive an hour late.* | 1. They got in a car accident.<br>2. They stood me up.<br>3. They ran out of gas. | Why were you late? | 1. We had a flat tire.<br>2. We got lost.<br>3. We <u>said</u> we'd be here at <u>7 o'clock</u>. |
| *You ask your parents to take you to the mall and they say NO!* | | | |
| *You see your boy / girl friend talking to someone else and they exchange phone numbers.* | | | |
| *Someone tells you gossip about a friend.* | | | |
| | | | |
| | | | |

**DON'T FALL IN THE TRAP.....**

## ASK – DON'T ASSUME!

**I. PURPOSE:**

To increase assertive skills by encouraging ''asking'' and discouraging ''assuming''.

**II. GENERAL COMMENTS:**

The trap of ASSUMING and not ASKING frequently gets people into uncomfortable situations. Often, incorrect assumptions are made. ASKING requires thought, time, and practice and will result in increased assertiveness. This is often a difficult task for students as they are frequently told NOT to ask any questions both at school and at home. It is recommended that some time is spent on discussing ''I'' statements in order to effectively complete the ''YOU ASK'' column.

**III. POSSIBLE ACTIVITIES:**

    A.  1.  Discuss all new or challenging vocabulary.

         2.  Use the example provided to explain the concept. Encourage discussion around the statement that ''Even kids have the ability and the opportunities to be ASSERTIVE''.

         3.  Encourage students to fill in the blank boxes as a class activity.

         4.  Encourage role-playing for the remaining situations. Review pages 7 & 8. Discuss how each communication style character might respond in these situations.

         5.  Process the right to ask questions and possible benefits.

    B.  1.  Divide the class into teams of three students. Student #1 writes reply in ''Your Assumption'' column and passes it to Student #2, who writes reply in ''You Ask'' column and passes it to Student #3 who writes reply in ''Possible Responses'' column. Inform them that they will be asked to share their responses when the class reconvenes.

         2.  Instruct students to rejoin the class.

         3.  Encourage each small group to share one or two favorites.

# SAYING "NO"

I. PURPOSE:

To increase assertiveness by recognizing certain situations in which it is difficult to say "no", and rehearsing and listening to "no" in an assertive style.

II. GENERAL COMMENTS:

A nonassertive communication style often results in a reluctant "yes", a mixed message, and/or a hostile "no".

III. POSSIBLE ACTIVITIES:

A. 1. Distribute handouts and discuss all new and challenging vocabulary.
   2. Instruct the students to read each example and to add their own thoughts and/or experiences on the spaces provided below each example.

   3. Brainstorm and complete the handout with other examples.

   4. On the space provided to the left of each letter, rate the examples 1-9 with #9 being the LEAST difficult and #1 being the MOST difficult.

   5. Tabulate the results, asking how many students rated example "A" as the most difficult, etc. Look for commonalities in occurrence. Ask the class why most people rated example "A", "B", etc., as most difficult, least difficult, etc.

   6. Review guidelines and example formats.

   7. Choose two students to role-play each example, demonstrating assertive behavior. If necessary, review the three communication styles. Encourage feedback from the class after the role-play.

B. 1. Review handout. Instruct students to check which situations are particularly difficult for them and to include any other examples. Encourage them to share.

   2. Distribute slips of paper and instruct students to write other personal examples in which they have difficulty saying "no". Collect and put in "hat".

   3. If necessary, review the three communication styles. Ask students to choose one slip from the hat and role-play, demonstrating assertive behavior.

   4. Encourage role-plays as a way to practice behavior. Expect that older students may test and accept their right to say "no", and turn down this opportunity to role-play.

   5. Encourage feedback from class.

   6. Process the importance of saying "no" in an assertive way.

# SAYING 'NO"

## YOU HAVE THE RIGHT TO SAY NO!

## DO YOU HAVE TROUBLE SAYING "NO" TO....

_____ A. ) your mother? *(e.g., who always asks YOU, and not your brothers or sisters, to do chores around the house)* _____
_____

_____ B. ) your teacher? *(e.g., who always asks you to run errands, collect papers, help other students)* _____
_____

_____ C. ) a fellow student? *(e.g., who always asks for the answers to a homework assignment, wants to copy off your paper)* _____
_____

_____ D. ) your siblings? *(e.g., who want to borrow your clothes, books, tapes, or who are always talking on the phone)* _____
_____

_____ E. ) your boy/girlfriend? *(e.g., who is jealous and possessive)* _____
_____

_____ F. ) door to door people? *(e.g., other kids selling candy, salespeople, fundraisers, charity collectors)* _____
_____

_____ G. ) a friend? *(e.g., who wants you to use drugs/alcohol with him/her, wants to borrow money/your car)* _____
_____

_____ H. ) a neighbor? *(e.g., who wants you to watch her five children "for just an hour", forgets to pay you or doesn't pay you enough for babysitting)* _____
_____

_____ I. ) _____

_____ J. ) _____

## GUIDELINES FOR SAYING "NO":
Be honest, open and direct.
Don't make excuses.

### Remember, by saying "no", you're gaining self-respect!

## EXAMPLE FORMATS...
No, I am unable to do that today. Maybe you can ...
No ... to be honest, I don't want to ...

I. **PURPOSE:**

To increase assertive skills by recognizing the right to change a situation.

To identify specific areas of potential change.

II. **GENERAL COMMENTS:**

Oftentimes, people in crisis think they have no choices. It takes time and effort to confront difficult situations and consider changes.

III. **POSSIBLE ACTIVITIES:**

A. 1. Provide the following example:

SITUATION: My parents don't give me an allowance.

CHANGE (NEGATIVE): I can refuse to do my homework until they reconsider their decision.
I can argue with their decision.
I can argue with them.
I can take money from their wallet/purse.

2. Distribute the handout. Discuss any new or challenging vocabulary. Encourage students to discuss the illustration and its relevance to the subject of change and choices. Discuss the differences between negative and positive responses to a situation. Present the example again.

SITUATION: My parents don't give me an allowance.

CHANGE (POSITIVE): I can get a part-time job and receive my own paycheck.
I can earn money from my parents by doing chores.
I can ask them to reconsider their decision by presenting them with a compromise.

3. Instruct students to complete the handout.

4. Ask one student to volunteer and share his/her work with the class, eliciting feedback and assistance to complete the handout if needed. Encourage the student to choose the best or most realistic option. Allow the students to assist each other in listing different situations and possibilities for change.

5. Process benefits of recognizing the right to change a situation and identifying specific areas of potential change. Process the benefits of eliciting support from others when deciding on changes.

B. 1. Discuss topic of the assertive right to change a situation. Discuss the difference between negative and positive responses to a situation.

2. Brainstorm on chalkboard possible situations or areas in need of change.

FOR EXAMPLE:
a) school
b) money
c) friends
d) family
e) relationships
f) environment
g) appearance
h) personality
i) stress level
j) living arrangements

3. Divide class into small groups of three students each, and provide each group with one copy of the handout.

4. Instruct each group to choose one category of change listed on chalkboard (refer to examples in B.2.).

5. Encourage students to work together to identify three situations within their category which need change (each student needs to contribute one situation). Encourage students to assist each other in listing possible ways to change each situation. Allow 15-20 minutes.

6. Reconvene as a class and share responses.

7. Process benefits of recognizing the right to change a situation and identifying specific areas of potential change. Process benefits of eliciting support from others when deciding on changes.

# I HAVE THE RIGHT TO CHANGE A SITUATION.

## I WILL EXPLORE OPTIONS & RESPECT MY CHOICES.

| SITUATION: | SITUATION: | SITUATION: |
|---|---|---|
| _____ | _____ | _____ |
| _____ | _____ | _____ |
| CHANGE: | CHANGE: | CHANGE: |
| A. _____ | A. _____ | A. _____ |
| _____ | _____ | _____ |
| B. _____ | B. _____ | B. _____ |
| _____ | _____ | _____ |
| C. _____ | C. _____ | C. _____ |
| _____ | _____ | _____ |

## I AM ABLE TO FEEL BETTER ABOUT MYSELF
## AS I CONSIDER THESE
## CHANGES!

# ASSERTIVE RIGHTS

I. PURPOSE:

To increase assertive skills by recognizing assertive rights.

II. GENERAL COMMENTS:

Assertive rights are often overlooked. Many people were never taught these *rights* as children, and many are in relationships infringing on these *rights*. Recognizing and exercising these assertive rights empower people, offering a sense of control and dignity.

III. POSSIBLE ACTIVITIES:

A. 1. Review prior basic vocabulary associated with assertiveness.

2. Distribute handout and discuss all new or challenging vocabulary.

3. Encourage each student to choose one *right* and explain it to the class, stating why it's important and ways to exercise that *right*.

4. Instruct each student to complete the handout by adding any *right* that they feel needs to be recognized.

5. Consider as a follow-up activity, role-playing the ''difficult'' assertive *rights* and processing the benefits of exercising these *rights*.

B. 1. Distribute handouts.

2. Discuss concept of assertive *rights*. Make an analogy with the Bill of Rights and their assertive *rights*.

3. Instruct students to check off those *rights* that are difficult for them to accept and live by.

4. Encourage each student to read aloud those statements s/he has checked, beginning with ''I, _____, have the *right* to _____''.

5. Ask each student to conclude with one goal based on their assertive *rights* checklist.

6. Encourage applause for efforts after each group member shares.

7. Direct the class to follow-up this activity with an entry in their diaries.

8. Process benefits of this activity.

# ASSERTIVE RIGHTS

Include these *rights* in your everyday thinking and gain self-respect, as well as respect from others.

I have the right to . . .

1. ___ say "NO".

2. ___ be competent and proud of my accomplishments.

3. ___ say "I don't know, I don't agree, and I don't understand".

4. ___ be treated with respect.

5. ___ express my needs, opinions, thoughts, ideas, and feelings.

6. ___ recognize MY needs as important.

7. ___ feel and express anger.

8. ___ have a support system.

9. ___ _____

10. ___ _____

# *ASSERTION* diary

## I. PURPOSE:

To increase assertive skills by observing, recording, and evaluating responses in various situations.

To identify alternative assertive responses.

## II. GENERAL COMMENTS:

Assertive skills allow for more effective communication. On a daily basis, one is given numerous opportunities to be assertive. Some interactions are handled assertively, thereby enhancing relationships and positively affecting self-esteem; others are handled in a passive or aggressive way, possibly harming relationships and lowering self-esteem. Diaries assist in the assessment process by allowing the individual to 1) recall interactions throughout the day, 2) record them in a logical, organized way, 3) evaluate them, and 4) identify alternative responses.

## III. POSSIBLE ACTIVITIES:

A.  1. Review prior discussion of assertion, discussing how it improves communication and relationships.

2. Distribute handouts. Discuss all new or challenging vocabulary.

3. Provide the following example to the class.

| Opportunity To Be Assertive | My Response | Feelings as a Result | Was I Satisfied? | Other Possible Assertive Responses |
|---|---|---|---|---|
| When the sales clerk at the department store continued with a personal phone call for several minutes while I waited to be assisted with my purchase. | I said nothing. I just stood there waiting. | Angry. Resentful. Irritated. Frustrated. | ☐ Yes<br>☐ Somewhat<br>☑ No | "Excuse me, I need some help. Do you have this in my size in another color?"<br><br>"Hello, I'm here to make a purchase. Could you help me find my size?" |

4. Instruct class to complete handout with 5 examples that have occurred within the past week. Encourage class brainstorming to assist students who might be having difficulty in completing the handout.

5. Ask class to share 2-3 of their examples, as time permits, and encourage feedback and support from others.

6. Process benefits of using a diary to increase assertive skills.

B.  1. Photocopy 7 handouts per student and staple in packets.

2. Provide overview of assertion, discussing how it improves communication and relationships. Include a discussion of the many opportunities available for assertion daily. Briefly discuss purpose of diary and benefits.

3. Distribute one packet per student.

4. Instruct group members to complete the first diary handout for today.

5. Share as able.

6. Instruct students to use remaining 6 sheets as daily diaries. Schedule class time daily for this activity. If possible, follow through during next class session.

7. Process benefits of using a diary to increase assertive skills.

# ASSERTION diary

| OPPORTUNITY TO BE ASSERTIVE | MY RESPONSE | FEELINGS AS A RESULT OF MY RESPONSE | WAS I SATISFIED WITH MY RESPONSE? | OTHER POSSIBLE ASSERTIVE RESPONSES |
|---|---|---|---|---|
| | | | ☐ Yes ☐ Somewhat ☐ No | |
| | | | ☐ Yes ☐ Somewhat ☐ No | |
| | | | ☐ Yes ☐ Somewhat ☐ No | |
| | | | ☐ Yes ☐ Somewhat ☐ No | |
| | | | ☐ Yes ☐ Somewhat ☐ No | |

# Self-Disclosure

Complete the following statements to gain an increased understanding of your SELF. You may want to DISCLOSE these thoughts and feelings to someone special to enhance your relationship.

- I am most content when _____

  _____

- My hopes and dreams for the future are _____

  _____

- I like myself most when _____

  _____

- I like myself least when _____

  _____

- My greatest fear is _____

  _____

- I feel disappointed when _____

  _____

- People think I am _____

  _____

- I value most _____

  _____

- One negative trait about myself is _____

  _____

- One positive trait about myself is _____

  _____

I'm going to share these thoughts and feelings with _____.

# Self-Disclosure

## I. PURPOSE:

To promote self-disclosure with others in order to improve communication skills and strengthen relationships.

To increase self-awareness and self-understanding.

## II. GENERAL COMMENTS:

Acknowledging and understanding one's own values allows greater potential for self-disclosures and honest communication between individuals. Self-understanding has the potential to positively influence relationships.

## III. POSSIBLE ACTIVITIES:

A.  1. Prepare activity by photocopying one handout and cutting it into ten strips of paper from the ten open-ended statements. Fold, and place in hat.

   2. Discuss all new or challenging vocabulary. Generate discussion regarding the effects and benefits of self-disclosures with communication and relationships.

   3. Encourage each student to choose a strip of paper from the hat, read it aloud and complete the self-disclosure statement. Return slips to hat when finished.

   4. Continue with all students for a designated time period.

   5. As a closure, ask all students to identify one significant person they plan to share their self-disclosure with, and how it might affect that relationship.

   6. Process benefits of this activity.

B.  1. Distribute handouts, encouraging students to complete the sentences, writing their responses on the lines provided.

   2. Facilitate a discussion of each statement, encouraging individuals to share.

   3. As a closure, ask all group members to identify one significant person they plan to share their self-disclosure with, and how it might affect that relationship.

   4. Process benefits of this activity.

# WOULDA SHOULDA COULDA

| | What are some self-defeating statements that you make? | How can you *reframe* these as positive self-talk statements? |
|---|---|---|
| **WOULDA** | | |
| **SHOULDA** | | |
| **COULDA** | | |

# WOULDA SHOULDA COULDA

## I. PURPOSE:

To increase communication skills by developing an awareness of self-defeating statements.

To learn how to reframe self-defeating statements for increased personal strength and self-control.

## II. GENERAL COMMENTS:

The "WOULDA... SHOULDA... COULDA" habit places unneccessary pressures on an individual. These statements are often made *after* an event has taken place and the situation cannot be changed. Rather than blaming oneself over a past event, new healthier ways can be identified to perceive the situation. "Reframing" allows the same subject to be viewed differently — the "old frame" is self-defeating, and the "new frame" enhances self-esteem. It is helpful to remind group members that a person does the best s/he can, given the awareness s/he has at *that* time.

## III. POSSIBLE ACTIVITIES:

A. 1. Introduce topic. Discuss all new or challenging vocabulary.

2. SELF-DEFEATING STATEMENTS:

   *(Personal)*
   If only I "coulda" stayed on my diet.

   *(Educational)*
   I "woulda" done better on that test, if only I had gotten enough sleep the night before.

   POSITIVE SELF-TALK STATEMENTS:

   Now I know what binge foods to avoid, in order to eat more nutritiously.

   I did my personal best.

3. Distribute handouts encouraging students to complete. Ask students to choose one area where they use self-defeating statements most often: in school, at home, with friends, at work, etc.

4. Facilitate discussion of volunteered responses.

5. Process benefits of this activity.

B. 1. Distribute handouts. Discuss all new or challenging vocabulary.

2. Discuss the "WOULDA...SHOULDA...COULDA..." habit, its effect on an individual's self-esteem and stress level.

3. Ask for examples of each of the three types of self-defeating statements presented in the handout, demonstrating possible ways to reframe.

4. Instruct students to complete handout by writing 3 different examples from their personal lives.

5. Ask each group member to read one statement from each category, giving first the self-defeating version and second, the reframed version.

6. Process benefits of this activity.

# COMMUNICATION BUILDING BLOCKS

# COMMUNICATION BUILDING BLOCKS

## I. PURPOSE:

To increase an awareness of verbal, nonverbal and 2-way communications.

To promote open communication.

## II. GENERAL COMMENTS:

Open communication which promotes verbal, nonverbal and 2-way communications offers the clearest "picture" to the receiver. Effective communication promotes improved personal and professional relationships.

## III. POSSIBLE ACTIVITIES:

A.  1. Discuss the communication model. In order to have two-way communication, there must be 4 essential parts: a sender, a receiver, a message and a response. If any component is missing, then there is ineffective communication. Ask the students to cite examples of mechanical means of one-way communication, e.g., T.V., radio, a public address system. Ask the students to cite examples of two-way communication, e.g., the telephone, two-way radio, CB, telegraph, walkie-talkies, direct face-to-face communication.

2. Photocopy 1 handout.

3. Distribute blank paper and pencils to all students.

4. Ask for a volunteer and instruct him/her (without showing the handout to others) to . . .
    a. choose one shape from the handout.
    b. describe it to the class using verbal cues only, so the others can accurately draw it on their papers. Use one-way communication only. Do not allow any questions/comments from the class. Do not use nonverbal cues (hand motions, body gestures, etc.).

5. Encourage students to show their drawings to the describer to compare their copies with the original.

6. Continue the activity by instructing volunteer #2 to describe a different shape verbally, but this time including nonverbal cues as well. Use one-way communication only.

7. Encourage students to draw, and then show their drawings to the describer to compare their drawings to the original.

8. Continue the activity by instructing volunteer #3 to describe a third shape verbally and nonverbally, allowing for two-way communication with group members.

9. Process the group by discussing students' reactions and responses to each of the 3 exercises, emphasizing the benefits of verbal, nonverbal and two-way communication.

B.  1. Photocopy one page and make cards of each of the twelve designs.

2. Give one card each to twelve students. Instruct each student, in turn, to describe their card to the rest of the class. They can choose to describe their cards . . .(a) verbally, with no nonverbal cues; (b) verbally and nonverbally, allowing no questions; or (c) verbally and nonverbally, encouraging questions.

3. Process the group by discussing the students' reactions to the exercise, and emphasizing the benefits of open communication.

# YOUR BODY CAN SPEAK

Your body has a language of its own.
Take a look at your body and the message you're sending to others.

## Your Eyes

Attempt to be at eye level when communicating with others. Remember, maintaining good eye contact is important. Be aware of eyebrow gestures.

_____

_____

_____

Attempt to keep all facial muscles relaxed. Avoid tightening your jaw, clenching your teeth, and fidgety movements. It is recommended that the facial expression reflect the feeling you wish to communicate.

_____

_____

## Your Facial

## Expression

## Your Shoulders

## and Arms

Attempt to keep shoulders straight and back, arms relaxed and uncrossed. Avoid overuse of shoulder shrugging.

_____

_____

_____

Attempt to keep handshakes firm and decisive. Remember... not too long, not too short, not too rough, not too flimsy!!

_____

_____

## Your

## Handshake

## Your Total Body

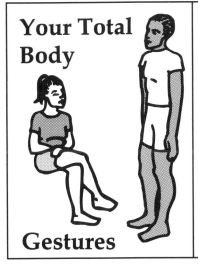

## Gestures

Attempt soft, smooth motions, instead of quick, abrupt ones. Be aware of personal comfort zones and maintain adequate distances. Turn your entire body, and "face" the person you're communicating with directly.

_____

_____

_____

_____

_____

_____

I.  PURPOSE:

To increase effective communication skills by recognizing and improving nonverbal messages.

II.  GENERAL COMMENTS:

Communication is a vital key to meaningful and successful interactions and relationships. Nonverbal communication can be extremely powerful in setting the stage for effective communication.

III.  POSSIBLE ACTIVITIES:

A.  1.  Discuss the potential for positive and negative messages to be sent nonverbally by demonstrating to the class the same message using assertive body language and nonassertive body language, (e.g., walk up to a student, put hand on his/her shoulder and with a smile, ask to see them after class. Approach another student, but this time stand with arms crossed or on hips, feet far apart, and ask him/her the same question, this time with a very stern facial expression.) Instruct class to process the difference in the two different situations. What message was given to the first student? What message was conveyed to the second student through the use of body language?

2.  Distribute handouts and discuss new or challenging vocabulary.

3.  Set up didactic role-plays using the following situations, demonstrating both positive and negative messages:
    a) ask teacher/counselor/clergy for time to talk.
    b) discuss possibilities of an increased allowance with parents or a raise with boss.
    c) confer with teacher about low grade.

4.  Elicit feedback from students after role-play. Ask students to describe specific physical messages sent and how this affected role-plays.

5.  Process benefits of recognizing and improving nonverbal messages.

B.  1.  Discuss concept of body language.

2.  Brainstorm on chalkboard the body language which accompanies assertive, passive, and aggressive communication, respectively.

3.  Divide class into small groups.

4.  Instruct groups to do mini-interviews with their partners. Each student is to first attempt assertive body posture during the interview and then accept feedback from his/her partner. Instruct class to follow this format:
    a) exchange names.
    b) complete this sentence, "One thing I'm looking forward to is _____."
    c) discuss two pieces of personal information (background, family, age, educational goals, etc.).
    d) give a handshake.

5.  Reconvene as a class. Encourage group members to introduce their partners to the class.

6.  Encourage feedback from the group about the introductions.

7.  Process benefits of recognizing and improving nonverbal messages.

8.  Distribute handouts. Ask students for additional insights and information as to age-related body language.

# Down in the dumps ? ?
# What Can You Do ? ? ? ?

# LIGHTEN UP ! ! !

### Remember . . .
## Even winners have to battle the blues!

## Which do you imagine yourself doing when you need to cope?

| | | |
|---|---|---|
| ASSERTING MYSELF | *or* | ASKING SOMEONE FOR HELP |
| CHANGING A HABIT | *or* | HELPING SOMEONE |
| GOING SHOPPING | *or* | LISTENING TO FAVORITE MUSIC |
| EATING SOMETHING HEALTHY | *or* | EXERCISING |
| TAKING A WALK | *or* | TAKING A BREAK |
| LEARNING SOMETHING NEW | *or* | GOING TO A MOVIE |
| WRITING A LETTER OR IN A JOURNAL | *or* | READING A BOOK/MAGAZINE |
| TALKING ON THE PHONE | *or* | TALKING TO A COUNSELOR |
| TAKING A HOT BATH/SHOWER | *or* | LAUGHING/CRYING |

## <u>Recognizing</u> the importance of these valuable tools is the first step in establishing coping skills. The next step is <u>exercising</u> these skills when feeling depressed, to increase your sense of well-being!

*Down in the dumps ? ?*

# LIGHTEN UP ! ! !

I.  PURPOSE:

To develop effective coping skills by identifying specific strategies to cope when feeling depressed.

II.  GENERAL COMMENTS:

When feeling depressed, there is an overwhelming sense of sadness that often inhibits development and/or implementation of coping skills. It takes effort, motivation and/or support to identify specific strategies to cope, but they offer a sense of control and optimism for the future.

III.  POSSIBLE ACTIVITIES:

A.  1.  Ask the class to explain to what *down in the dumps* refers. Remind the class that everyone *gets the blues* once in a while. Assure them that this is a healthy and normal human emotion. Also assure them that *feeling blue* doesn't last forever. Can they explain the statement "Even winners have to *battle the blues*"?

What does the light bulb represent? What happens to a darkened room when a lamp is turned on? Discuss the analogy of a light bulb in a darkened room and individual coping skills when you're *feeling blue.*

2.  Provide a brief explanation of the benefits of developing individual coping skills.

3.  Distribute handout and discuss new or challenging vocabulary.

4.  Instruct students to choose one from each pair and complete by writing as many ideas of coping behaviors as they have.
    For example:
    Asserting myself: "Sharing my feeling of loneliness with best friends."

    Changing a habit: "I'll only watch 2 hours of TV rather than my usual four or more each night."

5.  Encourage students to self-disclose as able.

6.  Discuss benefits of having a plan of specific strategies to cope when feeling depressed.

B.  1.  Provide a brief explanation of the benefits of developing individual coping skills.

2.  Photocopy handout and cut into 36 cards.

3.  Place cards in center of table or desk. Ask a volunteer to choose a card and describe to the class how s/he might use that coping skill. Students can *pass* on one card if they are unable to answer, and give it to the person on the right. They must choose the next card, however, and answer it.

4.  Process benefits of having a plan of specific strategies to cope when feeling depressed.

# LIMITS

1

2

3

4

By setting these limits, I am taking more control of my life, increasing my self-esteem, and establishing boundaries in my relationships.

Signature:

_____

# LIMITS

I. PURPOSE:

To increase coping skills by identifying benefits of setting limits.

II. GENERAL COMMENTS:

Limit setting establishes necessary personal boundaries. Vague limits often produce stress and anxiety. The ability to set limits is effective with oneself, and with others, in every area of life. The benefits of setting limits include increased sense of control, increased self-esteem and stress management, and improved quality of relationships... just to name a few!

III. POSSIBLE ACTIVITIES:

A. 1. Distribute handout. Discuss new or challenging vocabulary.

2. Ask students why people put up signs? Ask them to recall signs that they have seen. What signs, if any, have they ever had to make for themselves? If there was one sign that they could create that could change their lives, for the better, what would it say?

3. What is the significance of the sign on this handout?

4. Inform them that the purpose of this activity is to become aware of how people, situations, and responsibilities can interfere with personal needs being met. In turn, feelings of anger and resentment result with a decreased sense of control and decreased self-esteem. Instruct the students to create their own "limits sign" using the language of assertion.

5. Ask students to set two limits from each category. List the following on the chalkboard.
   a) Relationships with...
      1. parents
      2. siblings
      3. neighbors
      4. friends
      5. boyfriend/girlfriend
      6. teacher
      7. self
      8. strangers

   b) Activities related to...
      1. extracurricular activities
      2. home
      3. finances (money)
      4. education
      5. leisure
      6. self
      7. church/synagogue
      8. community

6. Remind the class to be as specific as possible, e.g., rephrase limits such as: "I will not be stepped on by my friends", to "I will limit the time I spend helping my friends with their homework to one hour a week."

7. Encourage class to share as able.

8. Process how limit setting is an effective coping skill.

B. 1. Distribute handouts.

2. Brainstorm all possible relationships and activities which may need limit setting. List on chalkboard.

3. Instruct students to write 4 limits on their handouts.

4. Ask students to role-play or state goals related to their identified limits.

5. Encourage students to share as able.

6. Process how limit setting is an effective coping skill.

# LOOK FOR ALTERNATIVES
## WHEN ROADBLOCKED!

IN A "STEW"?
① Identify your problem.
② Identify your roadblock.
③ Look for alternatives!

PROBLEM:

ROAD-
BLOCK:

## REMEMBER...YOU HAVE ALTERNATIVES!

# LOOK FOR ALTERNATIVES

I. PURPOSE:

To improve coping skills by recognizing potential roadblocks and by identifying possible options.

II. GENERAL COMMENTS:

When inundated by problems, it is easy to lose perspective and not see what the roadblocks are, or what the alternative choices might be. Identifying options is one effective coping skill.

III. POSSIBLE ACTIVITIES:

A. 1. Discuss new or challenging vocabulary.

2. Offer the following example or try to elicit one from the class:

PROBLEM: My grades in all my subjects are slipping.

ROADBLOCK: I use my freetime at school and at home for activities other than completing my homework.

ALTERNATIVES: I will study as soon as I get home.

I will ask my parents for help.

I will ask my teachers if extra help is available, especially during study hall.

3. Distribute handouts and encourage class to complete the handouts individually. Ask the class for suggestions if anyone might be experiencing difficulty with the handout.

4. Facilitate discussion of individual's options, encouraging class to offer feedback.

5. Discuss benefits of this skill.

B. 1. Distribute handout and ask each student to write a problem which s/he is experiencing.

2. Pass them to the right or mix them up and pass them around, and ask each student to select one. Instruct each one to read aloud, in turn, the problem and identify possible solutions. Ask the class for feedback or suggestions.

3. Return papers to original owners and ask if any of the solutions seem feasible to them.

4. Process benefits of looking at options and receiving ideas from others when facing a difficult problem.

# M O T T O

# GAME

| | | | | |
|---|---|---|---|---|
| "HASTE MAKETH WASTE." | "A watched pot never boils." | *"Time flies when you're having fun."* | "An apple a day keeps the doctor away." | "Busy hands are happy hands." |
| "One day at a time." | "All work and no play makes Jack a dull boy." | "Just say NO." | "DON'T BURN THE CANDLE AT BOTH ENDS." | "Never put off til tomorrow what you can do today." |
| *"Don't count your chickens before they hatch."* | "Live and learn." | "STICKS AND STONES MAY BREAK MY BONES BUT NAMES WILL NEVER HURT ME." | *"That's what friends are for."* | "All for one and one for all." |
| "Better late than never." | "THE BEST THINGS IN LIFE ARE FREE." | "No one is an island." | "Don't cry over spilt milk." | "To err is human. To forgive divine." |
| "A friend in need is a friend indeed." | *"You're never too old to learn."* | *"A penny saved is a penny earned."* | "Procrastination is the thief of time." | *"Two heads are better than one."* |
| "You can't unscramble eggs." | "MANY HANDS MAKE LIGHT WORK." | "Take time to smell the roses." | "EARLY TO BED, EARLY TO RISE..." | "Don't sweat the small stuff." |
| "IF IT WORKS, DON'T FIX IT." | *"Look before you leap."* | "Honesty is the best policy." | "First things first." | *"To thine own self be true."* |

## I. PURPOSE:

To increase coping skills by adopting WELLNESS MOTTOS as personal mottos.

## II. GENERAL COMMENTS:

It is easy to overlook the wisdom that lies within these mottos. Reminiscing, discussing, thinking, and laughing assist in the integration of these thought-provoking mottos.

## III. POSSIBLE ACTIVITIES:

A.  1. Discuss all new or challenging vocabulary.

   2. Photocopy 2 copies of the handout. Mount them onto a piece of tagboard. Cut into 70 cards. Number the back of each card from 1 to 70. (For younger students, use less cards, but be certain that you have one pair of each motto.)

   3. Turn the cards face down on a table or desk. Divide the class into two teams. Play "Concentration" where one member of Team #1, in turn, calls out two numbers. Each card is uncovered and the team tries to make a match. Turn the cards face down if they do not match. Team #1 scores a point for each correct match. Allow the teams to lend support to their respective teammates. Remove each matching pair from the playing area. Award Team #1 a bonus point if they can correctly explain the motto. If not, the opposing team can try to guess the motto and earn a bonus point. Team #1 continues its turn until they fail to make a correct match. The turn then switches to Team #2.

   4. Play until all the cards have been correctly matched and uncovered.

   5. Process favorite/most meaningful mottos, encouraging group members to adopt mottos to assist with coping.

B.  1. Make a bingo card master with 5 blank blocks horizontally and 5 blank boxes vertically. Fill in the "Free Space" and photocopy as many copies as needed. Distribute one blank bingo sheet to each student.

   2. Before class, cut markers out of heavyweight paper. Make enough so that each student receives 25.

   3. Also prepare beforehand, flash cards with each motto on the card.

   4. Select one motto one at a time, read it to the class, and ask for a volunteer to explain it. Instruct the class to write the motto in any blank box anywhere on the card. Continue until all the boxes on the handouts are filled. Using the flashcards, play "Motto Bingo". The winning student must select their favorite motto and explain what it means and why it is an important motto.

   5. Process by asking class how adopting mottos can be an important coping skill. Encourage students to adopt at least one motto. Permit students to keep their motto cards.

# BLACK W IT

BLACK and WHITE thinking leaves the whole world of GRAY out in the cold.
Try experimenting with gray thinking.

## WHITE

## BLACK

*I hate myself when I goof up!*

*I become impatient with myself when I make mistakes.*

## BLACK

## WHITE

EVERYBODY   ANYTHING   NOBODY   NEVER
ALWAYS   EVER   EVERYONE   NOTHING

## I. PURPOSE:

To facilitate learning and self-discovery (1) by recognizing "absolute" or "all-or-nothing" statements, and (2) by learning how to neutralize them.

## II. GENERAL COMMENTS:

"Black & white thinking" refers to "absolutes" or "all-or-nothing" statements. Many students (especially those who are participating in concerned persons groups), demonstrate "black & white thinking" and oftentimes extreme behavior is associated with this. Reframing the words or phrases such as those noted on the bottom of the handout, promotes neutralizing or blending of "black & white thinking" into "gray thinking".

## III. POSSIBLE ACTIVITIES:

A. 1. Discuss new or challenging vocabulary.

2. Distribute handouts. Explain topic with discussion of concept. Explain how "black & white thinking" creates limits. Demonstrate how acting in accordance with true wishes is stopped by "black & white thinking". Tension is generated causing avoidance of an activity in the future. Facilitate discussion of what is implied when an absolute is used in self-descriptions.

3. Discuss where "black & white thinking" may stem from, e.g., parents, teachers, siblings, the media, friends, past experiences.

4. Discuss example on handout.
ABSOLUTE - "I hate myself when I goof up."
NEUTRAL - "I become impatient with myself at times."

5. Instruct class to write 3 more examples of their own "absolutes" or "all-or-nothing" statements. Encourage students to reframe those statements into neutral messages.

6. Encourage students to offer one example from their handouts to the group for feedback.

7. Process benefits of this activity.

B. 1. Before class, prepare card game by writing those "absolute" statements/phrases from bottom of handout several times each to make a deck of 30 cards.

2. Discuss concept of "black & white thinking" with students eliciting personal examples.

3. Instruct each student to choose a card and identify a time/situation in which s/he may use that statement/phrase, giving a specific example.

4. Ask students to choose another student to reframe the "absolute" for him/her.

5. Continue until all have chosen a card and all students have been asked to reframe.

6. Process benefits of identifying "black & white thinking" and receiving feedback on ways to reframe.

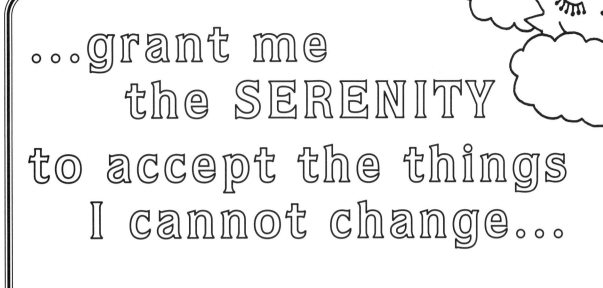

...grant me
the SERENITY
to accept the things
I cannot change...

_____

_____

_____

COURAGE to change
the things I can...

_____

_____

_____

and the WISDOM to
know the difference.

I.   PURPOSE:

To promote boundary recognition as a step to recovery.

II.  GENERAL COMMENTS:

Tangible, concrete work with this theme reinforces its powerful message.

III. POSSIBLE ACTIVITIES:

A.  1. Distribute handouts. Discuss new or challenging vocabulary.

    2. Instruct class to complete mini-posters with marking pens, colored pencils or crayons. (Completed works can be used for a cover of a folder or as a wall hanging in classroom.)

    3. Process the activity by reinforcing the importance of the serenity theme.

B.  1. Distribute handouts.

    2. Instruct students to complete mini-posters with marking pens, colored pencils or crayons. (Completed works can be used for a cover of a folder or as a wall hanging in classroom.)

    3. Divide group into two smaller groups.

    4. Instruct one group to list and discuss things (personal issues, topics, situations) they _cannot_ change. As an additional activity for a future group, refer to WOULDA... SHOULDA... COULDA, page 15, using this _cannot change_ list.

    5. Instruct the second group to list and discuss things (personal issues, topics, situations) they _can_ change. As an additional activity for a future group, refer to SEALS PLUS UNIT 6 - GOAL SETTING pages 29-33, using this _can change_ list.

    6. Reconvene the class and share results.

    7. Process benefits of this activity.

# eMotiONS

| | | | | | | |
|---|---|---|---|---|---|---|
| aggressive | alienated | angry | annoyed | anxious | apathetic | bashful |
| bored | cautious | confident | confused | curious | depressed | determined |
| disappointed | discouraged | disgusted | embarrassed | enthusiastic | envious | ecstatic |
| excited | exhausted | fearful | frightened | frustrated | guilty | happy |
| helpless | hopeful | hostile | humiliated | hurt | hysterical | innocent |
| interested | jealous | lonely | loved | lovestruck | mischievous | miserable |
| negative | optimistic | pained | paranoid | peaceful | proud | puzzled |
| regretful | relieved | sad | satisfied | shocked | shy | sorry |
| stubborn | sure | surprised | suspicious | thoughtful | undecided | withdrawn |

## I. PURPOSE:

To increase awareness of emotions and a variety of words to express emotions, with assistance of visual representations.

To increase usage of these words.

## II. GENERAL COMMENTS:

Identifying emotions is an effective communication skill. Everyday language can be enhanced by using the most specific word to describe feelings at any time. This allows the "receiver" to get a clearer picture of what the "sender" is trying to say and increases the chance of a more effective response.

## III. POSSIBLE ACTIVITIES:

A. 1. Discuss new or challenging vocabulary. Keep a dictionary or thesaurus readily available for clarification of terms as necessary.

2. Discuss the value of being able to identify emotions and to express them. Possible answers are:

   If I'm honest with myself I can be more honest with others,
   I can be closer to others,
   I can ask others for what I need,
   I will feel more alive and energized, etc.

3. Distribute handout. Instruct students to select their favorites and to discuss why they like them. Is it due to the feeling expressed or is the illustration pleasing? Ask them to identify their least favorite emotions. Why are they their least favorite?

4. Ask them to identify which feelings they might have experienced during the ages listed below:

   Birth - 5 years
     6 - 11 years
   12 - 17 years
   18 - ?

5. Before class, make one photocopy of the handout, cut out each emotion and attach to an index card. Instruct each student in sequence to select an emotion card from the deck and share it with the group using one of the following formats:

   "I feel _____ when _____."

   or

   "The last time I felt_____ was when _____."

6. Encourage this process to continue until all emotions are discussed from the handout.

B. 1. Make a card game by cutting each of the 63 emotions out of one handout and attaching each on a separate index card. Place in a "hat".

2. Divide class into two teams.

3. Encourage one student from team #1 to choose a card and pantomime the emotion for team #2, then team #2 guesses which emotion it is. This handout can be given to all group members to assist them.

4. Score by giving one point for correct response given within 60 seconds.

5. Repeat process with team #2 pantomiming for team #1.

6. Continue game until time runs out or all cards are played.

7. Process the importance of using specific words to express emotions.

# "I feel..."

. . . two powerful words when used together to assert yourself. Personal power is lost when you say *"you make me feel"* instead of saying *"I feel".*

Make a list of common situations in which you give up or have given up control by blaming others for your feelings. Then rewrite the situation using this suggested approach beginning with "I feel". Recognize how accepting responsibility for your feelings can change the way you view a situation.

| "You make me (feel)..." | "I feel..." | "Since I'm in control of my feelings, my choices are..." |
|---|---|---|
| *You make me feel uncomfortable at parties when you drink.* | *I feel uncomfortable at parties when you drink.* | *I can go and be miserable/turn my attention to others/leave the party/not go to the next one.* |
| *You make me angry when you don't listen.* | *I feel angry when you don't listen.* | *I can continue "as is" with resentment/ask you to set a specific time to talk/ask you to give some response (nod, eye contact, "okay").* |
| | | |
| | | |
| | | |
| | | |

# "I feel..."

## I. PURPOSE:

To increase emotion identification by gaining experience and knowledge using "I feel" statements.

To recognize options as a result of being in control.

## II. GENERAL COMMENTS:

Increased control and responsibility are felt when one states "I feel". "You make me feel" is a communication "bad habit" which gives control to the other person. "I feel" is, in essence, stating "I choose or allow myself to feel," thus giving increased choices to the individual.

## III. POSSIBLE ACTIVITIES: This handout can be used in conjunction with EMOTIONS (page 24).

A. 1. Discuss new or challenging vocabulary.

2. Review topics covered in ASK – DON'T ASSUME, page 9 and LIMITS, page 19. Distribute handouts and explain concept by reading top portion of handout and two examples.

3. Encourage group members to complete page using personal examples. If students are experiencing difficulty in completing handout, encourage students to assist one another or give them the following examples:

STUDENT TO PARENTS: You make me feel embarrased when you call me by my nickname in front of my friends.
STUDENT TO TEACHER: You make me feel resentful when you compare me to my older brother or sister.
STUDENT TO SIBLINGS: You make me angry when you borrow my clothes, books, etc., without asking.

4. Discuss and encourage students to share as able the following topics:

(a) Assertive people take responsibility for their own thoughts, feelings and actions. They respect others who do the same.
(b) Even when we are unsure of what we are feeling, we can still express what we are aware of with "I . . ." statements.
(c) "You make me . . ." statements blame and accuse the other person.
(d) We make our own choices on how to react or respond. Even if we feel unable to change some things, other people do not have control or power over us.

5. Process the use of an "I feel" statement as one assertive principle.

B. 1. Distribute slips of paper and encourage each student to jot down three personal examples of situations in which they have said "You make me feel". Place in "hat".

2. Instruct students to choose one.

3. Encourage role-playing of each situation.

4. Process benefits of assertive expression of feelings.

# INSIDE OUTSIDE

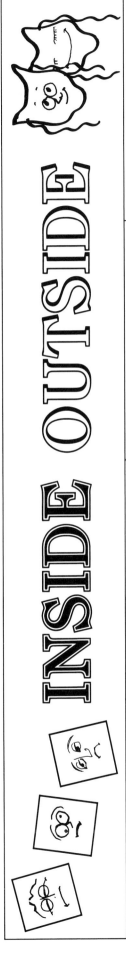

| Name a situation in which you experience grief. | "Inside, I feel…" (*only I* know that I am feeling…) | "Outside, I appear…" (*other people view me as…*) | Outcome/results of inside/outside differences. |
|---|---|---|---|
| | ☐ aggressive ☐ alienated ☐ angry ☐ annoyed ☐ anxious ☐ apathetic ☐ bored ☐ cautious ☐ confident ☐ confused ☐ depressed ☐ determined ☐ disappointed ☐ discouraged ☐ disgusted ☐ embarrassed ☐ envious ☐ exhausted ☐ fearful ☐ frustrated ☐ guilty ☐ happy ☐ helpless ☐ hopeful ☐ hostile ☐ humiliated | ☐ hurt ☐ hysterical ☐ innocent ☐ jealous ☐ lonely ☐ loved ☐ miserable ☐ negative ☐ optimistic ☐ pained ☐ paranoid ☐ peaceful ☐ puzzled ☐ regretful ☐ relieved ☐ sad ☐ shocked ☐ shy ☐ sorry ☐ stubborn ☐ surprised ☐ suspicious ☐ thoughtful ☐ undecided ☐ withdrawn ☐ _____ | ☐ aggressive ☐ alienated ☐ angry ☐ annoyed ☐ anxious ☐ apathetic ☐ bored ☐ cautious ☐ confident ☐ confused ☐ depressed ☐ determined ☐ disappointed ☐ discouraged ☐ disgusted ☐ embarrassed ☐ envious ☐ exhausted ☐ fearful ☐ frustrated ☐ guilty ☐ happy ☐ helpless ☐ hopeful ☐ hostile ☐ humiliated | ☐ hurt ☐ hysterical ☐ innocent ☐ jealous ☐ lonely ☐ loved ☐ miserable ☐ negative ☐ optimistic ☐ pained ☐ paranoid ☐ peaceful ☐ puzzled ☐ regretful ☐ relieved ☐ sad ☐ shocked ☐ shy ☐ sorry ☐ stubborn ☐ surprised ☐ suspicious ☐ thoughtful ☐ undecided ☐ withdrawn ☐ _____ | ☐ Physical symptoms: _____  ☐ Behavioral symptoms: _____  ☐ Emotional symptoms: _____ |

While it *is* OK to have differences between our feelings and expressions, it is also important to recognize that the greater this difference, the greater the internal stress level. Bridging the gap between inside and out can be done in several ways. What are some of your ideas?

# INSIDE OUTSIDE

## I. PURPOSE:

To gain insight regarding the discrepancy between how one feels and what one expresses while experiencing grief.

To identify 1) the physical, behavioral, and emotional implications of the "Inside, I Feel..."/ "Outside, I Appear..." discrepancy, and 2) ways to bridge the gap of this discrepancy.

## II. GENERAL COMMENTS:

Oftentimes, people in grief feel that no one understands them. They often don't understand themselves. It might be due to discrepancies between emotion identification and emotion expression. It is vital to remind people that the greater the discrepancy, the greater the internal stress level. Further implications might involve...

    a) headaches, stomach problems, anxiety attacks.

    b) other people, due to reactions related to feelings from grief.

    c) confusion, frustration and/or ambivalence.

## III. POSSIBLE ACTIVITIES:

A. 1. Explain concept of "Inside, I Feel..."/"Outside, I Appear..." using the following example:

| Name a situation | Inside | Outside | Outcome/Results |
|---|---|---|---|
| anniversary of a loved one's death | [X] painful [X] confused [X] miserable [X] angry [X] annoyed [X] irritable | [X] hopeful [X] peaceful [X] determined [X] confident | physical: ulcer behavioral: relationship difficulties emotional: feel alone and     unsupported |

  2. Distribute handouts. Discuss new or challenging vocabulary. Instruct students to complete. If they are experiencing difficulty in recalling an instance when they experienced grief, encourage the students to share and to assist one another.
SUGGESTIONS: Students often experience grief if they or their friends must relocate to another community. They experience grief at the loss of a favorite teacher, pet, family member, neighbor. They experience grief leaving the elementary school environment and beginning junior high/middle school. If they have been in treatment for substance abuse, they lose their drug of choice, coping behaviors and peer group.

  3. Ask students to share, with emphasis on implications and ways to bridge the gap of this discrepancy.

  4. Process the activity.

B. 1. Explain concept of "Inside, I Feel..."/"Outside, I Appear..." using the following example:

| Name a situation | Inside | Outside | Outcome/Results |
|---|---|---|---|
| Possibility of not graduating | [X] angry [X] depressed [X] fearful [X] helpless [X] hostile [X] shocked | [X] determined [X] hopeful [X] optimistic | physical: migraine headaches behavioral: poor test results,     poor attendance,     homework not completed emotional: feel confused, exhausted,     resentful that others aren't more     sensitive to needs |

  2. Distribute handouts, instructing class to complete.

  3. Facilitate role-plays, by encouraging students to choose situations in which they were unable to express their grief well.

    For example: "My parents decided to separate, and my father would not be home when I came home from school. I became angry when a teacher asked me to do something, so I started an argument with him/her and was sent to the office for a discipline referral."

  4. Encourage students to first do the role-play as the situation actually happened, and then work on communicating their grief more effectively.

  5. Ask students to provide support and feedback for those who are role-playing.

  6. Process benefits of this activity.

# Experiencing a sense of loss?

# Grief grabs you when you're least prepared!

## Do you:

- ☐ start to say something and forget what it was you wanted to say?
- ☐ feel lonely even though you are in a room filled with people?
- ☐ feel overwhelmed with the flooding of many emotions?
- ☐ often misplace your books, keys, clothes, shoes, etc.?
- ☐ forget what you were about to do 5 minutes ago?
- ☐ become upset when watching TV or a movie; when reading a newspaper or a book?
- ☐ have a difficult time concentrating?
- ☐ cry for no apparent reason?
- ☐ feel cheated?
- ☐ feel a *twang* when you see a striking resemblance, a familiar hairdo, certain clothing?
- ☐ feel like staying in bed, or better yet, climbing under the bed?
- ☐ feel a sense of loss at Thanksgiving, birthdays, other holidays?
- ☐ feel someone's missing even though you are surrounded by loved ones?
- ☐ feel a tremendous sense of emptiness, void, or hole in your life?
- ☐ feel "shook-up" when you see a photograph unexpectedly?
- ☐ feel fine for a period of time, and get depressed again for no apparent reason?
- ☐ feel angry at your loved one whom you've lost, yourself, your family, or people who are trying to help you?
- ☐ feel as if your values have changed — things that used to be important to you aren't important anymore?
- ☐ feel as if you should look different to others, and are surprised that they can't see your sadness?
- ☐ other _____

## feel saddened when:

- ☐ it's the anniversary date of a birthday? death? divorce?
- ☐ you notice a familiar scent that reminds you of the past?
- ☐ you go to a certain restaurant? certain place? certain neighborhood?
- ☐ the seasons change?
- ☐ you see other kids' parents getting along well?
- ☐ you see a father and son, mother and daughter, siblings, best friends, etc., together?
- ☐ you hear a certain song? certain type of music?
- ☐ other _____

# . . . it'll get better . . . and if not better, it'll get different!

I.  PURPOSE:

To facilitate the grief process by:
1) acknowledging often unrecognized symptoms and feelings, and
2) recognizing benefits of discussing grief in a group setting.

II. GENERAL COMMENTS:

Grief is an intense feeling of deep sorrow and sadness caused by a loss. Oftentimes when people are experiencing grief symptoms, they are feeling alone, isolated, and unsupported. It is important for people who are grieving to realize that they are not alone and that there are common grief symptoms and feelings.

III. POSSIBLE ACTIVITIES:

A.  1. Review group rules. Reinforce the concept that within the class setting exists a safe environment for sharing.

2. Discuss new or challenging vocabulary.

3. Present concept of grief "grabbing" a person when s/he least expects it.

4. Discuss the concept that grief can be experienced not only at the death or loss of a loved one, but also through:
- divorce
- move or relocation
- friends', neighbors', significant others' relocation
- loss of a favorite teacher
- recovery from substance abuse
- parent's job loss
- graduation from school or leaving one school setting for another, e.g., private school to public school, elementary to secondary
- any response the students might offer

5. Distribute handouts and ask students to complete by identifying which situations have happened to them.

6. Discuss each situation, asking class to volunteer to share their experiences.

7. Pursue *other* comments, asking class to share what they have written.

8. Discuss last thought on the bottom of the page, ". . . it'll get better . . . and if not better, it'll get different", and ask class if they've noticed a difference as time has passed.

9. Process the benefits of recognizing grief symptoms and feelings, and discussing grief in a group setting.

B.  1. Present concept of grief "grabbing" a person when s/he least expects it.

2. Ask class to complete handouts by identifying which situations have happened to them.

3. Discuss each situation, asking a student to volunteer to share an emotion that co-exists with grief in that particular situation. Assist students by using a list of varied emotions. (See page 24-EMOTIONS).

4. Process the benefits of recognizing grief symptoms and feelings, and discussing grief in a group setting.

# SIGNIFICANT LIFE EVENTS

| Event | Age | EMOTIONS |
|---|---|---|
| | | |

# SIGNIFICANT LIFE EVENTS

I. PURPOSE:

To promote recall of positive and negative events which had a significant effect on one's life.

To increase self-awareness of emotions associated with significant life events.

II. GENERAL COMMENTS:

Taking an inventory of one's past can often increase insights regarding present attitudes and behaviors. By reminiscing or reviewing life events, one can evaluate past experiences, influences, and patterns. This can assist in determining future directions.

III. POSSIBLE ACTIVITIES:

A. 1. Discuss new or challenging vocabulary.

2. Introduce concept with the following examples or one of your own:

| Event | Age | Emotions |
|-------|-----|----------|
| divorce of my parents | 7 | anger, hurt, resentment, fear, relief |
| going to a new school | 11 | fear, anxiety, optimism, excitement |

\* Note: emphasize that at times we have mixed emotions about an event; emotions are not always all comfortable or all uncomfortable.

3. Encourage each student to complete the handout, depicting his/her own significant life events through words, pictures, symbols.

4. Instruct class to find a partner, and allow approximately 10-15 minutes for an "interview" of each partner.

5. Reconvene the class at the end of the "interview" and ask each student to describe his/her partner's significant life events.

6. Process by asking class to discuss insights gained from this activity.

B. 1. Introduce concept with the following examples or one of your own:

| Event | Age | Emotions |
|-------|-----|----------|
| divorce of my parents | 7 | anger, hurt, resentment, fear, relief |
| moving to a new house | 12 | fear, anxiety, dread, excitement |

\* Note: emphasize that at times we have mixed emotions about an event; emotions are not always all comfortable or all uncomfortable.

2. Divide class into small groups of 2 or 3. Distribute 1 handout to each group. Encourage group to choose a famous or meaningful character and complete the handout as if they were the character. For example:
a) Anne Frank
b) Tom Sawyer
c) Richard Nixon
d) Magic Johnson
e) Christopher Columbus

3. Instruct each group to choose a representative to share its group's findings.

4. Distribute handout and instruct each student to complete his/her own.

5. Encourage students to share as able.

6. Process benefits of this activity.

**GOAL SETTING** is one way to organize yourself and to get yourself moving in a positive direction.

# Must be...

REALISTIC &

# Can be...

| Career-oriented |
| :---: |
| Personal |
| Financial |
| Social |
| Educational |
| Other |

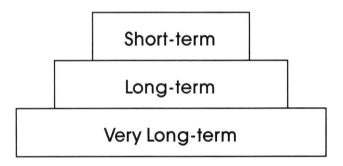

# Include...

1.  What goal you really want to accomplish.

   _____ .

2.  How you will evaluate/measure your progress.

   _____ .

3.  How much time it will take to reach this goal.

   _____ .

# GOAL SETTING is one way to organize yourself...

I. PURPOSE:

To increase knowledge about goals and benefits of goal setting, and to learn to apply this information.

II. GENERAL COMMENTS:

Setting goals and ultimately achieving them gives a sense of direction or control to an individual, which can lead to increased self-esteem. Be aware that the terms "short-term", "long-term", and "very long-term" are subjective and relative terms, depending on the age and grade level of the students.

III. POSSIBLE ACTIVITIES:

A. 1. Bring a small, empty, clear plastic container to class and enough marbles, jelly beans, chocolate kisses, etc., to fill it.

2. Discuss new or challenging vocabulary.

3. Distribute handouts. Discuss with class each type of goal in CAN BE section.

4. Demonstrate to the class how CAN BE section can be a combination of both columns, e.g., career-oriented short-term, career-oriented long-term, etc.

5. Using the analogy of a sports team, ask the class to surmise the team's goals using all possible combinations from the CAN BE column. Use examples from an individual player, the entire team and the manager's point of view.

6. Using the handout as a guide, instruct the class to create a class-wide educational goal, e.g., to see a movie, 45 minutes of computer time, etc. Then, instruct each student to write their own educational goals, e.g., to improve score on next spelling assignment by one letter grade.

7. Ask each student to share his/her goal. Collect the handouts and display in the classroom.

8. Each following day, ask students to share their goals with the rest of the class. At the end of the day and/or each time they achieve their goal, place a jelly bean, etc., in the jar. When the jar is full, the class receives their class goal, sharing the contents of the jar. A consequence for not achieving an individual goal can be the removal of a reward item, if desired.

9. Non-food rewards such as a poster with the class names, using stickers or stars, reward passes, etc., are suggested as an alternative.

B. 1. Write the following terms on index cards: realistic, measurable, career-oriented, personal, financial, social, educational, short-term, long-term, very long-term.

2. Encourage students to select a card and define the term in their own words.

3. Instruct students to create a goal based on the card they selected.

4. Process benefits of goal setting.

# Goal Setting
## Practice Sheet

**INCLUDE:** { **the task or goal you want to accomplish.**
**how it will be measured.**
**how long it will take to accomplish it.**

**EXAMPLES:** { I will _finish my science project_ with _a grade of 92%_ by _Friday of next week._
(task)　　　　　　　　　(standard)　　　　　　(time span)

I will _organize my room_ by _cleaning my closet_ before _this weekend._
(task)　　　　　　　(standard)　　　　　　　(time span)

## YOUR TURN:

#1 _____

| Can I really achieve this? *(realistic)*   YES ☐   NO ☐ |
| How will I know when I've achieved this? *(measurable)* |

#2 _____

| Can I really achieve this? *(realistic)*   YES ☐   NO ☐ |
| How will I know when I've achieved this? *(measurable)* |

#3 _____

| Can I really achieve this? *(realistic)*   YES ☐   NO☐ |
| How will I know when I've achieved this? *(measurable)* |

# Goal Setting
## Practice Sheet

I.  PURPOSE:

To practice "goal setting" by learning to use the 3 necessary criteria as indicated on top portion of this handout.

II.  GENERAL COMMENTS:

It takes practice to write realistic and measurable goals. Examples are included as a visual tool and reminder, but there are many other formats which are correct as long as they include the 3 criteria.

III.  POSSIBLE ACTIVITIES: This handout can be used in conjunction with GOAL SETTING IS ONE WAY (page 29) and/or GOALS (page 31).

   A.  1.  Distribute handout. Discuss new or challenging vocabulary.

   2.  Encourage students to complete handout with pencil (if goal is not realistic, it can be easily erased and rewritten).

   3.  Allow students to take turns reading their goals aloud, giving time for each to receive feedback.

   4.  Process the need for goal setting, writing goals and strategically placing them as a positive reminder.

   B.  1.  Encourage class to brainstorm possible goals on the chalkboard.

   2.  Address each goal one at a time, considering the 3 criteria.

   3.  Process the need for goal setting, writing the goals, and strategically placing them as a positive reminder.

# G⊙ALS

Name _____

GOAL _____
_____
_____
_____
_____
_____

GOAL _____
_____
_____
_____

GOAL _____
_____
_____
_____

GOAL _____
_____
_____

GOAL _____
_____
_____

## GOALS

I. **PURPOSE:**

   To encourage goal setting.

II. **GENERAL COMMENTS:**

   Writing goals, rather than just verbalizing them, is one way of increasing the likelihood of follow-through.

III. **POSSIBLE ACTIVITIES:** This handout can be used in conjunction with GOAL SETTING IS ONE WAY (page 29) or GOAL SETTING PRACTICE SHEET (page 30).

   A. 1. Review goal setting information.

   2. Encourage students to write 5 goals.

   3. Instruct students to choose one goal from their handouts and write it on the chalkboard, eliciting feedback from others.

   4. Process benefits of goal setting.

   5. Encourage students to place their goals in a highly visible location in the classroom to serve as a motivator.

   B. 1. Discuss with the class the definition and purpose of a resume.

   2. List on the chalkboard specific areas in the students' lives, where the goals they had set for themselves were accomplished.

   3. Ask the students to visualize a job or position that is very desirable. Instruct them to use the top half of the handout to write a career goal based on this ideal job. Ask them to share their ideas.

   4. Instruct each student to use the bottom half of the handout to list all previously achieved goals. The goals listed should be relevant to past accomplishments, achievements, strengths and skills needed to be hired for this ideal job.

   5. Choose two students to role-play the situation of an interview for the ideal job. Student #1 plays the role of the applicant; student #2 is the interviewer.

   6. Ask the students to perform the role-play, **without** the benefit of student #1's "resume". Re-create the role-play, this time, allowing student #1 to use his/her "resume".

   7. Process the benefits of goal setting and the disadvantages of not setting goals.

   8. For additional goal setting experience, photocopy as follows:

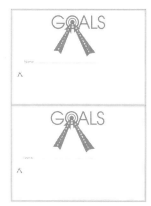

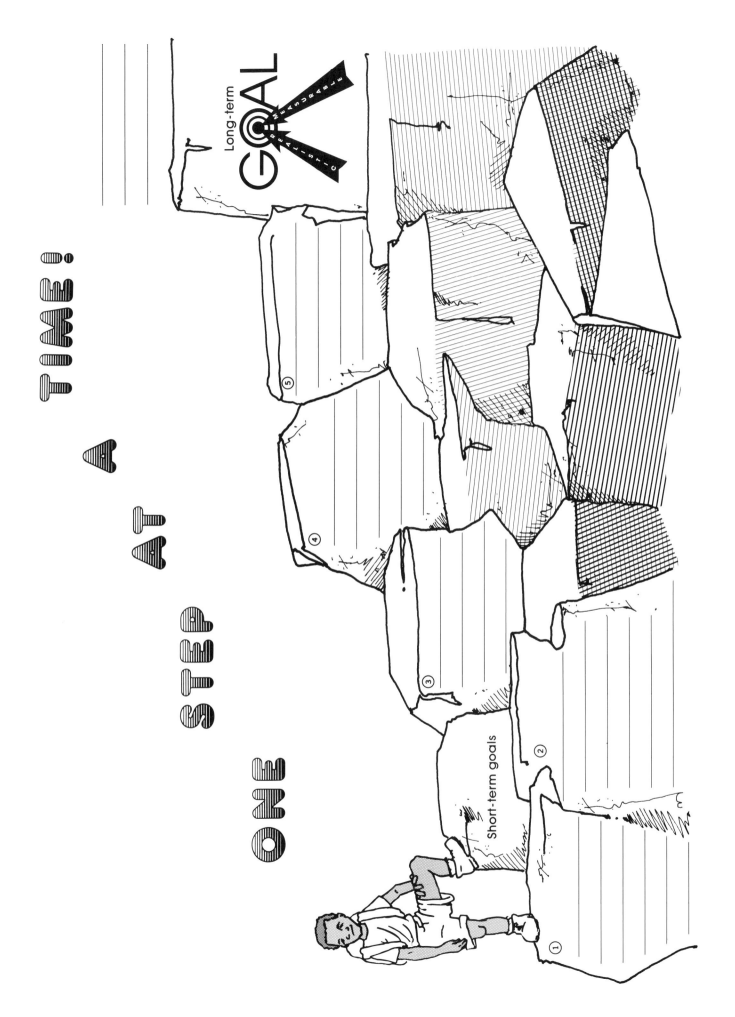

ONE STEP AT A TIME!

Short-term goals

Long-term GOAL
MEASURABLE
REALISTIC

# TIME!
## A
### AT
### STEP
# ONE

I. PURPOSE:

To gain an understanding regarding the importance of short-term goals in meeting long-term goals.

To gain experience in identifying and writing realistic short-term goals.

II. GENERAL COMMENTS:

Short-term goals can be viewed as "stepping stones" enabling one to meet a long-term goal. One way of recognizing progress toward a long-term goal is by acknowledging achievement of short-term goals.

III. POSSIBLE ACTIVITIES:

A. 1. Instruct students to write a long-term goal on the lines provided above the words "Long-term Goal", upper right of handout. The following example may be used: finish social studies report or pass test for learners driver permit.

2. Encourage students to write the first thing needed to be done in order to meet that long-term goal.
   stone #1, e.g., Make sure I understand assignment and am certain of date it is due.
   stone #2, e.g., Go to library.
   stone #3, e.g., Complete research notes.
   stone #4, e.g., Type paper, make a copy, include bibliography.
   stone #5, e.g., Give completed paper to teacher.

3. Ask students to share their examples and elicit feedback.

4. Process the value of short-term goals in conjunction with long-term goals.

B. 1. Give one stapled packet of 6 copies to each student, or divide the class into groups and give each group a packet.

2. Assign the following categories as goal topics:
   a. career
   b. personal
   c. financial
   d. social
   e. educational
   f. behavioral
   g. substitute any other that is relevant to age or grade level.

3. Instruct students to complete one handout per category. Long-term goals in Activity A, part 2, may be used as examples.

4. If time permits, request that the class reconvenes and shares their work. If necessary, continue discussion during next SEALS session.

5. Process the value of short-term goals in conjunction with long-term goals.

# REINFORCERS

## LIST 5 DESIRED TASKS, EXTERNAL REINFORCERS AND INTERNAL REINFORCERS.

| DESIRED TASK | EXTERNAL REINFORCERS | INTERNAL REINFORCERS |
|---|---|---|
| *I will complete all my math assignments this week.* | *I will buy myself a reward.* | *My stress level will decrease.* |
| | *After five school days, I will reward myself with one hour of a videogame.* | *I'll have more understanding of math.* |
| | | *I'll have a better relationship with my teacher/parent/guardian.* |
| | *I will earn better grades in math.* | *I'll experience a sense of accomplishment.* |
| | | *Lessened threat of repeating a grade or attending summer school.* |
| 1 | | |
| 2 | | |
| 3 | | |
| 4 | | |
| 5 | | |

# REINFORCERS

## I. PURPOSE:

To increase knowledge of external and internal reinforcers.

To commit to completing a desired task by creating external reinforcers and recognizing internal ones.

## II. GENERAL COMMENTS:

It is important to recognize **external reinforcers** as "outside influences" that one can implement to achieve a desired task, and **internal reinforcers** as "natural influences" that result as the desired task is achieved.

## III. POSSIBLE ACTIVITIES:

A. 1. Distribute handout. Discuss new or challenging vocabulary.

2. Explain concept of external/internal reinforcers using example provided. Ask students to share instances from their lives that are examples of external/internal reinforcers, e.g.,
   DESIRED TASK – to complete household chores;
   EXTERNAL REINFORCER – student will receive an allowance, room will be clean;
   INTERNAL REINFORCER – sense of accomplishment, knowledge that contribution
     is valuable.

3. Encourage students to fill in the five desired tasks and their external and internal reinforcers.

4. Facilitate discussion using the students' examples.

5. Process meaning of external and internal reinforcers and their importance.

B. 1. Distribute handout. Explain concept of external/internal reinforcers using example provided.

2. Encourage students to fill in five desired tasks and their external and internal reinforcers.

3. Collect handouts from all students.

4. Read one example from each handout encouraging members to guess the author and to elicit feedback.

5. Process meaning of external and internal reinforcers and their importance.

## SOFA-SPUD SYNDROME

Write your answer, **YES** or **NO** in the space provided:

_____ 1.) Do you have trouble getting up and leaving a comfortable place?

_____ 2.) Do you sit for endless hours in one place with no "get up and go"?

_____ 3.) Do you eat more junk foods or drinks than nutritious food?

_____ 4.) Are homework, reports, deadlines or household chores piling up?

_____ 5.) Are the television guide and remote control your BEST FRIENDS?

_____ 6.) Is the bathroom becoming a FOREIGN PLACE?

IF YOU ANSWERED <u>YES</u> TO 2 OR MORE OF THE ABOVE SYMPTOMS, YOU HAVE THE DREADED...
***SOFA-SPUD SYNDROME***. ALL KIDDING ASIDE, THE SOFA-SPUD SYNDROME HAS PRETTY
SERIOUS IMPLICATIONS: **POOR PHYSICAL AND MENTAL HEALTH!**

TRY ANSWERING THESE QUESTIONS TO HELP YOU MAKE A PLAN:

What can I *say to myself* to give me that "get up and go"? _____

What helps motivate me? _____

What limits can I put on my behavior? _____

What is one activity I can do after I "get up and go"? _____

Who can support me to "get up and go"? _____

Other ideas: _____

_____

SET A GOAL TODAY — MASH SOFA-SPUD SYNDROME!

# SOFA-SPUD SYNDROME!

I. PURPOSE:

To increase awareness of compromised activities of daily living (ADLs).

To problem-solve methods which promote higher functioning in ADLs.

II. GENERAL COMMENTS:

Lethargy impairs *all* occupational performance areas:
   work,
   self-care,
   and leisure,
however self-care skills are often compromised *first*.

The SOFA-SPUD SYNDROME is a light-hearted way to approach declining ADLs.

III. POSSIBLE ACTIVITIES:

A. 1. Distribute handouts. Discuss all new or challenging vocabulary.

2. Using illustration, facilitate a discussion of the definition and symptoms of SOFA-SPUD SYNDROME. Allow students to share their own symptoms of SOFA-SPUD SYNDROME.

3. Ask class to answer the six questions. Tally results. Ask the class to discuss the mental and physical health implications if most of the class answered "YES" 5 or more times, 4 or more times, etc.

4. Problem-solve using the "TRY ANSWERING THESE QUESTIONS" section.

5. If necessary, recall and review information discussed in COPING SKILLS (UNIT 4) and GOAL-SETTING (UNIT 6).

6. Instruct class to choose one question from the handout to which they answered "YES". Ask them to write a daily goal based on the question by selecting a healthier coping behavior.

7. Ask students to share their goals, eliciting feedback from the class.

8. Process effects that ADLs have on self-esteem, self-confidence and self-image.

B. 1. Distribute handouts.

2. Facilitate discussion of SOFA-SPUD SYNDROME.

3. Make 4 photocopies of the section "TRY ANSWERING . . ." and separate each question into a single strip. There are now 24 questions to place in a basket. (If class size is larger than 24, make enough copies so that each student has an opportunity to participate.)

4. Pass basket to the class so that each student takes one question. Present one problem area from the handout, for example: question 4—"*Are homework, reports, deadlines or household chores piling up?*"

5. Encourage turn-taking as students read their questions aloud and respond to the situation accordingly.

6. Assist each student to state response in terms of a concrete, short-term goal.

7. Process benefits of this activity.

# EXERCISE INTEREST CHECKLIST

It is well known that exercise is of benefit to everyone. Choosing which exercise to do is not an easy task! It depends on present physical condition, doctor recommendations (if necessary), personal likes and dislikes, etc.

Here's a list of choices. Put a "**P**" (present) in the first box if you presently do this two or more times each week. Put an "**F**" (future) in the second box if you are going to continue doing this or are considering doing this one or two times each week in the future.

| P | F | | P | F | | P | F | |
|---|---|---|---|---|---|---|---|---|
| | | Jogging | | | Bowling | | | Baseball / Softball |
| | | Walking | | | Yardwork | | | Roller / Ice-Skating |
| | | Running | | | Tennis | | | Soccer |
| | | Swimming | | | Racquetball | | | Volleyball |
| | | Bicycling | | | Weight Lifting | | | Football |
| | | Dancing | | | Stretching | | | Basketball |
| | | Aerobics | | | Aquatics | | | _____ |
| | | Downhill Skiing | | | Yoga | | | _____ |
| | | Cross Country Skiing | | | Work-out Machines | | | _____ |
| | | Water Skiing | | | Golf | | | _____ |

## List of "P"s

_____

_____

_____

_____

## List of "F"s

_____

_____

_____

_____

List 3 "**F**"s that you are not doing presently and identify what you'll need to do to GET STARTED.

1. _____

2. _____

3. _____

# EXERCISE INTEREST CHECKLIST

I. PURPOSE:

To take an inventory of present exercises and choose possible future exercises.

II. GENERAL COMMENTS:

Choosing the "right" exercise might be assisted by *reviewing* exercise choices, *selecting* realistic possibilities, and *discovering* what resources are available.

III. POSSIBLE ACTIVITIES:

A.  1. Discuss new or challenging vocabulary.

   2. Ask the class to share any example of something they once thought they wouldn't like or couldn't do, but once they tried, they were surprised to find it was pleasant or enjoyable. For example: using a computer, skiing, trying new foods, getting a hair cut. Accept other responses.

   3. Ask them to recall some of the thoughts or assumptions they had that held them back from participating, e.g., "I'm embarrassed", "it's too difficult", "I was afraid I'd look silly", "No one else was trying it."

   4. Write the word **EXERCISE** on the board. Ask the class to share their reactions to the word. Write their reactions on the board.

   5. Tally the number of negative reactions. Ask the class how these reactions affect desire and ability to exercise.

   6. Discuss myths about exercise. Possible answers might be:
      —makes you too muscular (for girls).
      —you perspire too much and could dehydrate.
      —it's bad for you to exercise too much.

   7. Discuss physical and mental benefits of exercise. Possible answers are:

| PHYSICAL | MENTAL |
|---|---|
| increases metabolism | improves mood |
| protects weight from "yo-yo" syndrome | increases energy |
| | reduces stress |
| healthier and longer life | |

   8. Ask the class to list what it takes to make the decision to exercise. What will be gained and what will be given up in order to begin an exercise regimen?

   9. Distribute handout. Reinforce that "P/F" is not the abbreviation for "pass/fail", but represents the terms "present & future".

   10. Instruct the class to complete handout, summarize their "P"s and "F"s, and list the resources where they can find "F"s.

   11. Process the benefits of choosing the "right" exercise regimen.

B.  1. Present handout as indicated.

   2. Encourage students to brainstorm and make a list of possible facilities that offer the activities listed.

   3. Provide adequate health and/or exercise reference materials. Instruct class to use the materials to locate information regarding each activity, for example: calories expended during activity, time required, special equipment required, etc.

   4. Divide list among class and instruct each student to call or write the facility to determine costs, times of day offered, location, and other information.

   5. Instruct class to bring information back to the next SEALS session and share.

   6. Process benefits of choosing the "right" exercise regimen.

# *Exercise Record*

**Name** _____    **Month** _____

| DATE | EXERCISE | TIME START | TIME END | TOTAL TIME | COMMENTS |
|------|----------|-----------|----------|-----------|----------|
|  |  |  |  |  |  |
|  |  |  |  |  |  |
|  |  |  |  |  |  |
|  |  |  |  |  |  |
|  |  |  |  |  |  |
|  |  |  |  |  |  |
|  |  |  |  |  |  |
|  |  |  |  |  |  |
|  |  |  |  |  |  |
|  |  |  |  |  |  |
|  |  |  |  |  |  |
|  |  |  |  |  |  |
|  |  |  |  |  |  |
|  |  |  |  |  |  |
|  |  |  |  |  |  |
|  |  |  |  |  |  |
|  |  |  |  |  |  |
|  |  |  |  |  |  |
|  |  |  |  |  |  |
|  |  |  |  |  |  |
|  |  |  |  |  |  |
|  |  |  |  |  |  |
|  |  |  |  |  |  |
|  |  |  |  |  |  |
|  |  |  |  |  |  |
|  |  |  |  |  |  |
|  |  |  |  |  |  |
|  |  |  |  |  |  |
|  |  |  |  |  |  |
|  |  |  |  |  |  |
|  |  |  |  |  |  |
|  |  |  |  |  |  |
|  |  |  |  |  |  |
|  |  |  |  |  |  |
|  |  |  |  |  |  |

## Exercise Record

### I. PURPOSE:

To establish a record-keeping system promoting a commitment to exercise.

### II. GENERAL COMMENTS:

Although most people realize exercise is of benefit, it is difficult to make a commitment to it. This handout enables people to visualize their accomplishments, which serves as motivation to continue.

### III. POSSIBLE ACTIVITIES:

A. 1. Explain concept of record keeping.

2. Distribute handouts. Discuss new or challenging vocabulary.

3. Instruct class that "COMMENTS" section may include:
   a. pulse rate before and/or after exercise
   b. physical response before and/or after exercise
   c. emotional response before and/or after exercise

4. Demonstrate to class the proper procedure for taking a pulse on the wrist or carotid artery. Instruct them to take their own pulse for 6 seconds. Take that number and add a "0" (zero) to the end of it to obtain pulse for one minute.

5. Lead the class for a walk around the school building, gym, playground or track. (Before this activity, ascertain the distance to be walked.) Instruct the class to be ready to record their physical and emotional responses.

6. Upon return to the classroom, instruct class to complete exercise record.

7. Discuss benefits of an exercise regimen and of record keeping.

B. 1. Distribute handouts. Explain concept of record keeping.

2. Instruct group members that "COMMENTS" section may include:
   a. pulse rate before and/or after exercise
   b. physical response before and/or after exercise
   c. emotional response before and/or after exercise

3. Discuss benefits of exercise.

4. Instruct class to:
   a. complete the handout by writing down all exercises (or lifestyle changes) within the time allotted.
   b. bring completed handout to next SEALS session.

5. Collect handouts and read aloud, encouraging students to guess the identity of the author.

6. Process the benefits of an exercise regimen and of record keeping.

# your eating habits

CHECK ALL APPROPRIATE BOXES:

■ ON AN EVERYDAY BASIS...

1. ☐ I eat one "fresh" fruit and one "fresh" vegetable.
2. ☐ For my age, height, body frame, and activity level, I have learned what my appropriate daily needs are to maintain or change my weight.
3. ☐ I control my calorie intake.
4. ☐ I am aware of and limit my cholesterol and fat intake.
5. ☐ I am aware of the possible effects of sugar and limit my sugar intake.
6. ☐ I am aware of my fiber intake.
7. ☐ I am aware of my calcium intake.
8. ☐ I regulate my caffeine intake.
9. ☐ I eat at least three times each day.
10. ☐ I eat slowly in relaxed, appropriate surroundings.
11. ☐ I concentrate on eating during mealtime and do not allow myself to become distracted.
12. ☐ My meals and table arrangements are carefully and thoughtfully planned in advance.
13. ☐ I drink at least eight 8-ounce glasses of water.

■ WITHIN THIS PAST WEEK...

14. ☐ I ate baked or broiled fish.
15. ☐ I ate oatmeal or stone-ground whole-grained bread or crackers.
16. ☐ I have tried 1 "new food" — (a food I <u>never</u> ate before).
17. ☐ I ate at a fast food restaurant no more than 1 time.

---

**SCORE:**  14-17 ✓'s — Wow for wellness!!! Wonderful!!!

8-13 ✓'s — Good, with a need for some improvement.

4- 7 ✓'s — OK...however, your work's cut out for you!

0- 3 ✓'s — Uh oh! Take care of yourself soon!

 your eating habits

## I. PURPOSE:

To take inventory of present eating habits, identifying areas for possible improvement.

To increase knowledge of nutrition.

## II. GENERAL COMMENTS:

Many factors influence wellness . . . positive eating habits are among them. Those listed in the handout provide a framework for education.

## III. POSSIBLE ACTIVITIES:

A. 1. Distribute handouts. Discuss new or challenging vocabulary.

    2. Divide class into small groups and work on each question, i.e.:
        8. I regulate my caffeine intake.
           Why?
           When?
           How?
           Which foods contain caffeine?
       16. I have tried one "new food".
           What?
           Where?
           Why is this important?
           New ideas?

    3. Invite a dietitian, nutritionist, health teacher, home economics teacher, or cafeteria supervisor to join the class and discuss principles covered in the handout. Discuss any alternative or healthier choices available. For example, substitute fruit for a candy bar, frozen low-fat yogurt for ice cream.

    4. Process benefits of positive eating habits.

B. 1. Encourage each student to complete the handout and score it.

    2. Facilitate discussion with the group noting areas checked and areas for improvement.

    3. Process benefits of positive eating habits.

# FOOD FOR THOUGHT

## At times, we eat in response to our emotions......

This association between eating and emotions may not interfere with healthy daily living, but at times it can lead to unhealthy behaviors.

**It may result in:**

- Overeating
- Undereating
- Not eating
- Making poor food choices
- Eating too quickly
- Purging after eating
- _____
- _____

Some of these behaviors can actually indicate or result in serious eating problems, requiring medical attention.

IT IS IMPORTANT TO RECOGNIZE WHEN YOUR EMOTIONS AFFECT YOUR EATING BEHAVIORS!

✓ one of the top bubbles, and then complete the rest of the cartoon.

☐ HMMMM.... IT'S MEAL TIME. WHY DON'T I FEEL LIKE EATING?

IF I EAT THIS, HOW WILL I FEEL IN AN HOUR? _____

☐ HMMMM.... I'M NOT REALLY HUNGRY RIGHT NOW. WHY DO I FEEL LIKE EATING?

MAYBE I FEEL... _____ BECAUSE I FEEL...

HOW ELSE CAN I COPE WITH THESE FEELINGS?

## Try to put things in perspective.

_Remember . . . we don't sleep every time we feel tired._
_Similarly, we don't need to eat, or not eat, every time we feel certain emotions._

**Do you respond to emotions through food?**

**Consider the following recommendations:**

- Recognize and allow yourself to feel your emotions, reminding yourself that these emotions won't last forever.
- Communicate your feelings openly and honestly with yourself and others.
- Look for alternative activities.
- Use positive self-talk.
- Relax, using methods you have found beneficial in the past.
- Use self-questioning methods —
  "Why am I eating this food?"
  "Why am I eating now?"
  "Why am I not eating at all?"
- Ask for help to create your own healthy food plan.
- _____
- _____
- _____
- If your eating behaviors are out of control. . .
  Seek medical assistance and counseling.
  Involve your family and/or friends to help.

# FOOD FOR THOUGHT

I. PURPOSE:

To recognize the relationship between eating and emotions. To identify the effect that emotions can have on eating behaviors, which can ultimately affect physical and emotional health.

II. GENERAL COMMENTS:

Eating or not eating can be a response to certain emotions. These emotions may be triggered by music, people, events, places, holidays, and thoughts about oneself or one's experiences, just to name a few. Physical and emotional well-being can be significantly affected.

III. SUGGESTED ACTIVITIES: This handout can be used in conjunction with EMOTIONS (page 24).

A. 1. Discuss new or challenging vocabulary.

2. Distribute one blank piece of typing paper to each student in the class.

3. Allowing only 3-4 minutes, instruct the class to create something using the piece of paper, other than using it to write or draw on. Some possibilities might be: a hat, an airplane, gift wrap, a bookmark, a sailboat, etc.

4. Ask the class to share their responses.

5. Recall prior discussions of emotion identification (Unit 5) and ask the class to list several emotions on the chalkboard.

6. Ask the class to discuss how emotions can/cannot manifest themselves (See GETTING TO KNOW YOUR ANGER, page 1, and/or INSIDE/OUTSIDE, page 26, for further clarification).

7. Instruct the class to make a comparison between the introductory activity and emotions. Focus the discussion on the concept that one traditional way of using paper is for writing or drawing. One traditional way of responding to emotions is eating or not eating. Just as the class can be creative and resourceful in using a piece of paper, they will be challenged to examine and develop new ways to cope with emotions other than eating or not eating.

8. Distribute handout and ask the class if they are aware of any emotions that are most likely to trigger an eating response, e.g., angry, anxious, bored, depressed, exhausted, happy, lonely, etc.

9. Draw the students' attention to the box on the left side of the handout. Discuss different ways that individuals choose to cope with their emotions by using or not using food. Additional possible responses might be: hiding food, secret eating, eating at times other than mealtime, eating in inappropriate places, e.g., the car, bus, in class.

10. Instruct the students to discuss the question of "Why do we use food as a coping skill?" Possible responses might be: it's socially acceptable; we need food in order to live; we need to eat at least three times a day; it's easily accessible; it's legal; it's warm, comforting, filling, tasty, gratifying, satisfying, etc.; it's a behavior, due to cultural or ethnic background, that's taught and accepted by my family; eating food can be a reward, or the denial of food can be a punishment; it's a distraction.

11. Draw the students' attention to the recommendations box on the right side. Discuss the recommendations and ask the class for any additions.

12. Instruct the class to complete the cartoon in the center of the handout using their own eating response to emotions.

13. Ask the class to share their responses as able, eliciting feedback.

14. Close by asking the class to summarize the activity. Allow each student to answer the following statement: "Next time I'm coping with my emotions by eating/not eating, I can choose to _____ instead."

B. 1. Follow steps 1-11 from Activity A.

2. Focusing the class' attention to the cartoon on the handout, note the two possible eating behaviors in response to emotions.

3. Divide the class into two groups.

4. Assign one group the role of top left bubble and the other group the top right.

5. Instruct each group to complete the cartoon according to their assigned role.

6. Allow 5-6 minutes for this activity.

7. Reconvene and ask one student from each group to share their group's responses, eliciting feedback from the rest of the class.

8. Ask the class to summarize the activity.

9. For further discussion, present the question: "How do emotions affect: speed of eating; food choices; where the food is eaten; when the food is most likely to be consumed; how food is eaten, e.g., while standing, out of a paper bag, a styrofoam container, etc.?"

10. Close by asking the class to summarize the activity. Allow each student to answer the following statement: "Next time I'm coping with my emotions by eating/not eating, I can choose to _____ instead."

# Sleep Well . . . z z z z

When restful sleep is not a consistent part of your lifestyle, check yourself out. These factors can influence your quality of sleep...

✔ one or more

☐ use of alcohol
☐ use of other drugs
☐ caffeine intake
☐ new medication
☐ illness

Sleeping environment:
☐ noise level
☐ temperature
☐ lighting
☐ visual surroundings

☐ stressors
☐ fluctuating sleep times
☐ lack of exercise
☐ eating habits
☐ Other _____

Now having identified the area(s) that may be affecting your restfulness, make a list of possible ways to counteract each factor.

| DESCRIPTION OF INFLUENCING FACTORS: | WHAT I WILL DO TO COUNTERACT THIS: |
|---|---|
| | |

# Sleep Well . . . $z^{z^{z^z}}$

### I.  PURPOSE:

To increase awareness of factors which may affect quality of sleep.

To identify ways to improve quality of sleep.

### II.  GENERAL COMMENTS:

Quality of sleep is determined by a combination of factors. It is valuable to evaluate present sleep patterns and habits, and identify a specific plan to counteract negative influences.

### III.  POSSIBLE ACTIVITIES:

A.  1.  Distribute handout. Discuss new or challenging vocabulary.

2.  Encourage students to complete handout.

3.  Make a card game by writing healthy and unhealthy sleep habits on separate index cards.

4.  Divide class into two teams.

5.  Instruct a student from Team #1 to choose a card from the stack and read aloud. Team #2 will be given 1 point if they can identify the habit correctly as healthy or unhealthy, and another point if they can explain why.

6.  Encourage teams to take turns until all cards are discussed or time is up.

7.  Applaud both teams for their efforts!

8.  Process benefits of healthy sleeping habits.

B.  1.  Distribute handout.

2.  Encourage students to complete handout.

3.  Discuss with students . . .
—checked boxes and any ''other''.
—description of influencing factors.
—counteractions.

4.  Process benefits of healthy sleeping habits.

# LEISURE WITHOUT LOSS . . .

...of $ $ $ that is!

Wellness! A balance of work, **leisure**, and self-care activities is one requirement for wellness.

Money is often a concern when engaging in leisure activities. Many leisure opportunities cost a great deal, but not all! Some of the most enjoyable experiences are free!

List below free (or almost free) leisure opportunities available to you.

_____     _____
_____     _____
_____     _____
_____     _____
_____     _____
_____     _____
_____     _____
_____     _____
_____     _____

Put a star ( ✳ ) by the five you will pursue.

How can you make these part of your life? _____

_____
_____
_____
_____

# LEISURE
# WITHOUT
# LOSS . . .

I. PURPOSE:

To increase awareness of available, free (or almost free) leisure opportunities.
To identify 5 inexpensive leisure activities that will be integrated into your lifestyle.

II. GENERAL COMMENTS:

A balance of work, **leisure**, and self-care is a requirement for wellness. However, leisure activities are often excluded from one's life due to financial stress. There is an unlimited number of opportunities available that do not cost anything (or cost very little).

III. POSSIBLE ACTIVITIES:

A. 1. Discuss new or challenging vocabulary.

2. Distribute handout. Discuss concepts of balancing work, leisure, and self-care. Discuss why this balance is important and the effect it has on mental and physical well-being. Use a scale, a simple lever and fulcrum, or a set of blocks to introduce and visually demonstrate the concept of balance.

3. Ask the class to identify the different types of work for which they are responsible. Responses will depend on age and grade level. Possible answers are: schoolwork, housework, babysitting, office paging, cafeteria helper, teacher's aide, etc. Demonstrate, using the visual aid, that all work and a lack of leisure, will create stress and unbalance in their lives.

4. Collect copies of local magazines, community newspapers, continuing education schedules, museum, fine arts, state park, zoo or extension service newsletters, and/or local library program schedules. Many weekend editions of local newspapers list free activities along with daily community calendars. Recycling or environmental organizations publish frequently. A wide range of free literature is available from your local public library. Make sure that copies of the telephone directory are available to the class during this activity.

5. Ask the class what they can do to create a balance of work and leisure. Recall previous discussion of SOFA-SPUD SYNDROME (page 34) and ask class to explain the difference between leisure time and SOFA-SPUD SYNDROME.

6. Brainstorm possible free (or almost free) leisure opportunities on the chalkboard. Instruct class to write the activities on their handouts as they are written on the chalkboard.

7. Distribute literature. Reassure the class that free (or almost free) activities do indeed exist. Instruct the class to use the literature to locate additional free (or almost free) activities.

8. Instruct the class to choose 5 from the list that they will pursue and highlight with a star (*) on their handouts.

9. Ask each student in turn to describe how s/he will incorporate these into his/her lifestyle. Brainstorm ideas for accommodating transportation problems.

10. Process benefits of leisure awareness.

B. 1. Write 20-40 free (or almost free) leisure activities on separate index cards.

2. Divide the class into two teams.

3. Select two members from each team to begin. Select one card from the deck and reveal it to one member of each team. Direct them to play "Password," by giving one word synonyms for the leisure time activity to their teammate. Point value begins at 10 points; for each additional synonym required, decrease the point value of each student's turn, until one point is reached. If the students are not able to correctly identify the leisure time activity, then ask the class to reveal the identity of the leisure time activity, no points awarded. After each leisure time activity is correctly identified, select four new players. Continue play until a predetermined score is achieved or until cards or time run out.

4. Suggest that the students jot down interesting leisure time activities on their handouts as they think of them during the game.

5. Conclude with a discussion focused on those written.

6. Process benefits of leisure awareness.

# MONEY MANAGEMENT

(or the lack thereof)

## Think about your spending habits and then circle (a) or (b):

1. **a.** I always buy anything I want.
   **b.** I only buy what I need.

2. **a.** I seldom spend money on leisure or entertainment.
   **b.** Leisure is important to me and I budget part of my money for it.

3. **a.** I put money in savings.
   **b.** I scrounge money weekly with nothing left over for savings.

4. **a.** If I buy a major item, I go to a store and buy it, saving time by not comparing prices.
   **b.** If I buy a major item, I compare prices, check into the best product, and then buy.

5. **a.** I save enough money to pay for items in full at the time I buy them.
   **b.** I must always borrow or ask for a loan in order to make purchases.

6. **a.** I can control cash in my hand / wallet, or I make sure I never carry too much cash.
   **b.** Cash is a "trigger" for me to spend.

7. **a.** I never spend money on myself.
   **b.** I choose to spend some money on myself.

8. **a.** I am always aware of how much money I make, spend and save.
   **b.** My money has a mind of its own; I allow my money to run itself.

9. **a.** I manage my money by myself — not asking for others' help.
   **b.** I ask for help from those who can manage money better than I.

10. **a.** I know how much money I have to spend and to save, and plan accordingly.
    **b.** I don't know my financial situation, so I don't plan.

 ***Which one of the above ten issues are you willing to work on?***

 ***What are potential outcome / results of these habits?***

## I. PURPOSE:

To increase awareness of personal spending habits.

To recognize areas of difficulty with money management.

## II. GENERAL COMMENTS:

Several factors affect the ability to manage or mismanage money. Some include:

1.) impulsivity,
2.) leisure values,
3.) ability to plan,
4.) organizing and planning,
5.) values regarding credit,
6.) immediate vs. delayed gratification,
7.) self-esteem/self-image,
8.) tendencies to avoid/confront,
9.) ability to manage money independently,
10.) awareness of financial situation.

These areas can be evaluated to increase an individual's awareness. Implications for change need to be considered.

## III. POSSIBLE ACTIVITIES:

A. 1. Distribute handouts. Discuss new or challenging vocabulary.

2. Ask students if they have ever played a board game involving planning and money management, e.g., "Monopoly" or "Life". Ask them to describe the rules for play. Both games involve successful planning and money management. Consequences of poor money management during play, result in bankruptcy and loss. Ask students to compare and contrast the board games to this activity.

3. Encourage each student to complete handout.

4. Discuss each question #1 through #10 with above outline.
See SECTION II. - GENERAL COMMENTS.)

5. Assist students in setting goals to change specific areas.

6. Process benefits of this activity.

B. 1. Photocopy handout and cut each question #1 through #10, parts a & b, into separate strips of paper (making 20 strips). Place in basket.

2. Encourage each student to take one strip from the basket and respond accordingly. Discuss as needed.

3. Distribute handout and encourage students to complete it. Assist students in setting goals to change specific areas.

4. Process benefits of this activity.

# BUYING HAPPINE$$ ?

**One coping skill that does not always work well is trying to "buy happiness".**
**This is just temporary...a Band-Aid. A shopping spree can lead to guilt,**
**the blues, embarrassment, unhappiness, stress, and perhaps debt.**

**Do you...**

1. binge-buy? (clothes, shoes, "sale" items) . . . . . . . . . . . . . . . . . . . . . . . . . . . . . yes ___ no ___

    the last time? _____

2. frequently loan or give money to friends (especially boy/girlfriends), knowing that they

    might never return or repay the loan?

    (even though you actually might need the money yourself?) . . . . . . . . . . . . . . . . . . yes ___ no ___

    the last time? _____

3. buy status objects? (name-brand items) . . . . . . . . . . . . . . . . . . . . . . . . . . . . . . . yes ___ no ___

    the last time? _____

4. buy impulsively? (clothing, gadgets, fad items) . . . . . . . . . . . . . . . . . . . . . . . . . . yes ___ no ___

    the last time? _____

5. spend excessively on others? (too expensive or too many gifts) . . . . . . . . . . . . . . yes ___ no ___

    the last time? _____

6. spend to escape unpleasant situations, e.g., arguing at home?

    (movies, videogame arcade, shopping at the mall) . . . . . . . . . . . . . . . . . . . . . . . . yes ___ no ___

    the last time? _____

**When/why do you do the above?** _____

_____

**What are potential implications of these habits?** _____

_____

The next time you feel the
urge to buy... take out this
wallet-size card and ask
yourself these questions
before you spend.

## BUYING HAPPINE$$ ????

Will I be pleased with my purchase
tomorrow... next week... next month... etc?

Am I able to afford this?

Do I want to spend my money on this right now?

Why am I REALLY buying this?

Am I OK with my reason for making this purchase?

# BUYING HAPPINE$$ ?

## I. PURPOSE:

To increase money management skills by:
1. recognizing self-defeating money management habits,
2. learning a self-questioning method to avoid these habits.

## II. GENERAL COMMENTS:

Oftentimes when depressed, anxious or stressed, it is a first impulse to SPEND in order to *buy happiness*. This "habit" or tendency is often self-defeating, leading to negative consequences.

## III. POSSIBLE ACTIVITIES:

A. 1. Discuss new or challenging vocabulary.

2. Conduct discussion on the interrelationship that money can have with emotional well-being. Write the statement, "Money can buy happiness" on the chalkboard. Encourage the students to respond, providing evidence either for or against the truthfulness of the statement.

3. List on chalkboard and discuss the meaning of the following 6 categories:

   binge-buying
   excessive loaning or borrowing
   buying status objects
   buying impulsively/on a whim
   overspending on others
   spending to escape unpleasant situations

4. Encourage students to:
   a. self-disclose as able, personal tendencies in, or examples of, each category.
   b. brainstorm list of whys, whens, and wheres.

5. Distribute handout.

6. Encourage students to complete the handout.

7. Review the self-questioning method as a coping behavior, discussing benefits.

8. Process benefits of this activity.

B. 1. Distribute handouts.

2. Explain interrelationship that money can have with emotional well-being.

3. Encourage students to complete handout.

4. Review self-questioning method as a coping behavior, discussing benefits.

5. Process benefits of this activity.

# OPENING DOORS TO ACHIEVEMENT

Don't allow obstacles to prevent achievements.
Confront these obstacles by doing the following:

| FILL IN POSSIBLE ACHIEVEMENTS | FILL IN POSSIBLE OBSTACLES | KEYS TO "UNLOCKING" THESE OBSTACLES |
|---|---|---|
| campaign for student government officer. | • fear of losing<br>• not enough time<br>• self-doubt | positive self-talk<br>ask for support<br>feedback from peers, family |
|  |  |  |
|  |  |  |

# OPENING DOORS TO ACHIEVEMENT

I. PURPOSE:

To increase problem-solving skills by gathering knowledge and experience in confronting obstacles.

II. GENERAL COMMENTS:

"Achieving" increases self-esteem. When one experiences difficulty in achieving, it is vital to recognize what may be preventing the achievement (obstacles) and the ways to remove/alter them (keys).

III. POSSIBLE ACTIVITIES:

A. 1. Use the following example to explain the handout:

| | | |
|---|---|---|
| • earning money | • I'm too young. | • positive self-talk, e.g., "Other people my age have jobs . . . babysitting, bussing tables at restaurants, yard work!" |
| | • I don't have references. | • I'll ask my teachers/counselors, etc., for a reference. |
| | • I get nervous when I have to ask for something, especially from a stranger. | • I'll ask my computer teacher to help me make a flyer to advertise myself. |
| | | • I'll practice interviewing with my homeroom teacher, counselor, etc. |

2. Encourage each student to complete handout. Encourage students to assist each other if they are having difficulty in completing the handout.

3. Process impact that problem solving and positive self-talk have on self-esteem and goal attainment.

B. 1. Write hypothetical "possible achievements" relevant to age and grade level on separate strips of paper and place in "hat".

2. Divide class into small groups of 2-3 students.

3. Instruct each subgroup to take one "possible achievement" from "hat" and as a group, problem solve with suggested technique from handout.

4. Facilitate discussion with entire class and encourage small groups to share their example.

5. Encourage students to complete handout, using a possible achievement from their own lives. Ask class to share as able.

# Positive Problem Solving
# Let's Brainstorm!

I.     Identify the problem: (specific) _____

II.    Be creative and list options and possible solutions.

☐ _____     ☐ _____

☐ _____     ☐ _____

☐ _____     ☐ _____

☐ _____     ☐ _____

☐ _____     ☐ _____

☐ _____     ☐ _____

☐ _____     ☐ _____

☐ _____     ☐ _____

☐ _____     ☐ _____

☐ _____     ☐ _____

III.    ✔ the boxes for those that sound reasonable to you.

IV.    Write in the three "best" and why you chose them.

     1 _____

     _____

     2 _____

     _____

     3 _____

     _____

V.     Review steps I, II, III, and IV once again and now decide on your plan.

_____

_____

_____

# Positive Problem Solving

I. PURPOSE:

To increase knowledge and gain experience in the problem-solving technique called "brainstorming".

II. GENERAL COMMENTS:

Often when confronted with a problem, it's difficult to see the alternative solutions, options, and possibilities. This technique affords creativity, increases choices, and improves the chances of decision satisfaction.

III. POSSIBLE ACTIVITIES:

A. 1. Distribute handout. Discuss new and challenging vocabulary.

2. Identify one specific problem on the chalkboard pertaining to all students in the class, e.g., I watch too much T.V. or I need to improve my study habits.

3. Present section II. Offer one option as a possible solution to the problem. Instruct the class to brainstorm other options and possible solutions. Encourage creativity by accepting all responses.

4. Proceed with sections III, IV, and V.

5. Facilitate discussion of sections I, II, and III.

6. Encourage students to complete handout individually.

7. Process strengths of this technique.

B. 1. Instruct class to complete handout, using one of their own specific problems.

2. Divide class into small groups of three to receive feedback from two other students on the completion of exercise.

3. Facilitate discussion with entire group as each student shares his/her problem and chosen plan.

4. Process importance of looking at all possible options before deciding on a plan to increase decision satisfaction. Discuss the idea that not all chosen plans will necessarily be the "right" ones, but may be the "best" ones at that time. Modifications may be made in the future.

# DECISION MAKING

You have the right to make decisions that involve challenges, opportunities, and risks.

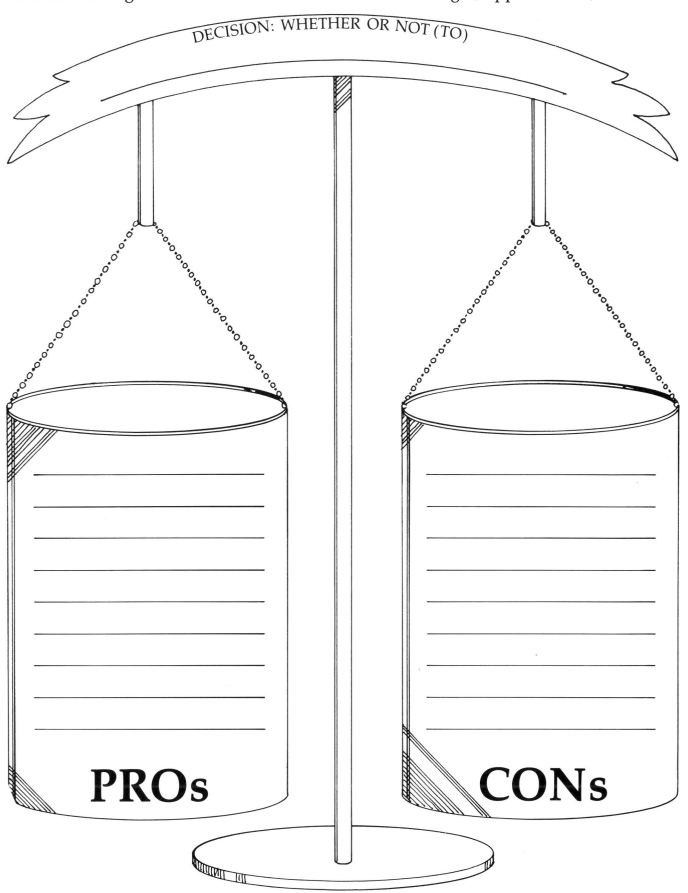

DECISION: WHETHER OR NOT (TO)

PROs

CONs

# DECISION MAKING

I. **PURPOSE:**

To increase decision-making skills by learning and experiencing the method of "weighing things out".

II. **GENERAL COMMENTS:**

It is easy to get overwhelmed with information when making a difficult decision. Internal conflict may arise when choosing the **best** option for yourself.

III. **POSSIBLE ACTIVITIES:**

A. 1. Discuss new or challenging vocabulary.

2. Present topic covered in handout by facilitating discussion of concepts in GENERAL COMMENTS section.

3. On chalkboard, introduce a classwide decision, e.g., to finish the social studies text by the end of the year, to go on a field trip, etc. Ask the class to first brainstorm any and all possible options. Discuss this process.

4. Present the issue again, first listing all the pros, then the cons. Discuss the advantages and/or disadvantages of this process.

5. Distribute handouts.

6. Instruct the class to fill in their own decision in the DECISION: WHETHER OR NOT (TO) space.

7. Encourage them to "weigh things out" by filling in the pros and cons, and then by taking a look at both sides of the issue.

8. Process the benefits of this decision-making method.

B. 1. Encourage students to brainstorm on the chalkboard, decisions students often face.

2. Choose one and use the method of "weighing things out" with the class.

3. Elicit feedback regarding the decision-making method.

4. Distribute handout. Instruct the class to complete as described. Collect handouts. Read the problem and the pros and cons. Encourage the class to guess what the writer decided, and/or the identity of the writer.

5. Process the benefits of using this decision-making method.

What's the worst thing that can happen if I try?

_____

If I never try, I'll never know if I can do it!

If I risk nothing, I risk...

_____

Why not?

Why not me?

Why not now?

_____

What have I got to lose?

_____

So, what's stopping me?

_____

Say "I can do it!"

Risk: _____

Say... "I WILL DO IT!"

"GOPHER" IT!

What's my risk?

_____

START

FINISH!

Plan: _____

# "GOPHER" IT!

## I. PURPOSE:

To promote risk taking.

## II. GENERAL COMMENTS:

The "go-for-it" pathway offers helpful questions and reminders inspiring a risk-taking attitude.

## III. POSSIBLE ACTIVITIES:

A.  1. Discuss new or challenging vocabulary.

2. Distribute handouts, read aloud or ask a student to read each step aloud, beginning at "start" and completing at "finish". Ask students to explain the meaning and/or the importance of each step by putting it into their own words.

3. Present a hypothetical opportunity for change, e.g., asking a teacher to reconsider a grade, or asking for extra help with an especially difficult assignment. Facilitate brainstorming of risks associated with the opportunity, by discussing each step from the handout from "start" to "finish".

4. Discuss artwork - why the steps are presented in a "horseshoe" shape.

5. Instruct the class to complete the handout using one risk of their own.

6. Encourage the students to share as able, eliciting feedback from other students.

7. Process value of risk taking.

B.  1. Instruct class to choose one risk they face and write it under the gopher.

2. Encourage students to write possible responses along the horseshoe, and then include a plan or goal on the bottom of the page.

3. Facilitate discussion as individuals share their plan or goal.

4. Process value of risk taking.

# To Risk or Not to Risk ???.....

..... Risk taking allows the opportunity for growth, change, and experience.....

..... Remember that to risk nothing in life is to risk everything.....

..... Self-esteem enhancement relies on challenging oneself to grow.....
therefore, to risk.....

..... Life is full of risks ready to be taken.....choices ready to be noticed.....
and skills ready to be strengthened.....

..... Which path will you follow?.....

---

**I have the opportunity to:**

1. take extra courses for high school college credit

2. _____

3. _____

---

|   | If I choose To Risk, then... | | If I choose Not To Risk, then... | |
|---|---|---|---|---|
|   | **I may gain:** | **I may lose:** | **I may gain:** | **I may lose:** |
| 1. | credits<br>experience<br>self-confidence<br>early graduation<br>new friends | time<br>leisure<br>friendships<br>tuition<br>grades might slip | time<br>increased leisure<br>no added stress<br>security<br>stability | adventure<br>new experiences<br>accomplishment |
| 2. | | | | |
| 3. | | | | |

# To Risk or Not to Risk ???.....

I. **PURPOSE:**

To promote decision making by evaluating risks to take and risks to decline.

II. **GENERAL COMMENTS:**

In every risk, there is something to gain and to lose. If no risk is taken, there is also something to gain and to lose.

III. **POSSIBLE ACTIVITIES:**

A. 1. Discuss new or challenging vocabulary.

2. Distribute handouts and ask the class to read each thought silently. Ask for a volunteer to then read each thought aloud, and discuss the meaning of each by rephrasing in his/her own words.

3. Explain the concept of risk taking with the following example on the chalkboard. Encourage discussion and feedback from the class.

| I have the opportunity to: *Audition for the school play/talent show* | | | |
|---|---|---|---|
| **If I choose to risk then,** | | **If I choose not to risk then,** | |
| I may gain: | I may lose: | I may gain: | I may lose: |
| experience<br>new friends<br>self-confidence<br>self-respect | time<br>comfort<br>old friendships<br>self-esteem<br>good grades<br>self-respect | time<br>increased leisure<br>no added stress<br>security/stability<br>comfort | adventure<br>new experiences<br>a sense of<br>   accomplishment<br>a challenge<br>self-respect |

4. Discuss example printed on handout.

5. Encourage class to describe similar hypothetical or possible risks that would be relevant to the entire class, e.g., trying out for a sports team, interviewing for a part-time job, etc., asking a teacher to reconsider a deadline or a grade. List all suggestions on the chalkboard.

6. Instruct the class to finish the second and third sections of the handout on their own, choosing two of the situations listed on the chalkboard.

7. Encourage them to share answers as able.

8. Process benefits of handout by eliciting feedback from students.

9. Close by asking students to volunteer to share one new thing that they learned from the activity.

B. 1. Encourage students to contribute hypothetical or possible risks, and write them on separate strips of paper. Put in "hat".

2. Instruct each student to choose one from the hat, using the situation to complete the second section of the handout.

3. Collect handouts and read aloud.

4. Instruct class to guess the author of each and offer feedback.

5. Process benefits of handout by eliciting feedback from class.

6. Close by asking for a student to volunteer to summarize the activity and to share what was learned.

# SHOOT FOR THE STARS!

SHOOT
FOR THE
STARS!

I. PURPOSE:

To set expectations which promote risk taking.

II. GENERAL COMMENTS:

Although goals need to be realistic and attainable, it is important to "set sights" high to ensure personal growth.

III. POSSIBLE ACTIVITIES:

A. 1. Select and become familiar with an easy biography of a popular celebrity, e.g., an Olympic athlete, famous newscaster, etc. Pass the book around to the class and permit students to **skim** through it. Ask the students to list, using a time line on the chalkboard, the accomplishments of this person's life.

2. Ask the class how this person was able to achieve fame, e.g., talent, hard work, parental sacrifices, scholarships, etc. Accept all responses.

3. Recall previous discussion of goal setting (see Chapter 6 pages 29-33). Relate concepts of goal setting to current discussion.

4. Instruct the class to discuss some of the **risks** this celebrity might have taken in accomplishing his/her goals. Discuss the **rewards** that this person has received.

5. Direct discussion to concepts listed in GENERAL COMMENTS. Use time line to illustrate.

6. Distribute handout. Encourage students to write 3 possible expectations, risks, beliefs and/or hopes based on personal situations.

7. Facilitate discussion using students' examples.

8. Process importance of self-growth and risk taking.

B. 1. Encourage students to write 3 possible expectations, risks, beliefs, and/or hopes.

2. Collect handouts and read aloud.

3. Encourage students to guess the author.

4. Elicit feedback from the class.

5. Process importance of self-growth and risk taking.

# RoLeS

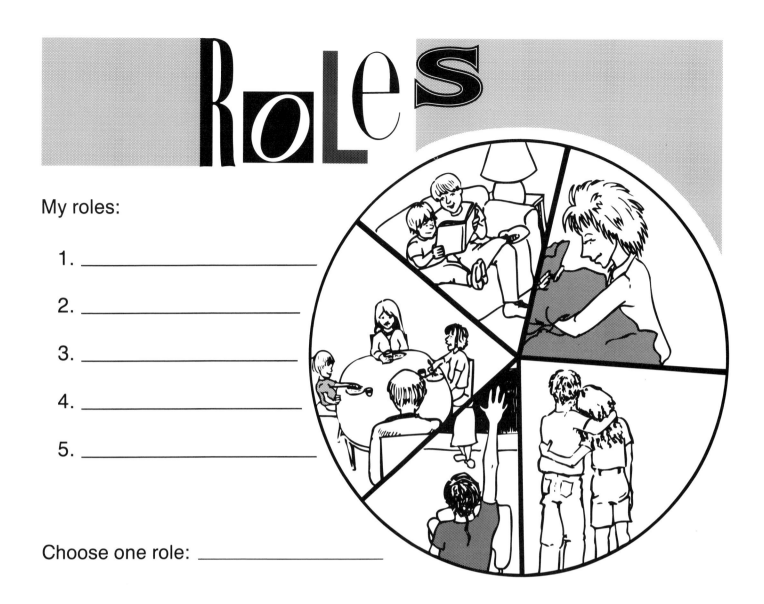

My roles:

1. _____

2. _____

3. _____

4. _____

5. _____

Choose one role: _____

| Things I do well within this role. **FOCUS ON POSITIVES!** | Things I don't do well within this role. **ROOM FOR CHANGE!** |
|---|---|
| 1. | |
| | |
| 2. | |
| | |
| 3. | |
| | |
| 4. | |
| | |
| 5. | |
| | |

Roles

## I. PURPOSE:

To acknowledge one's present roles in life.

To focus on what one does well within these roles.

To recognize areas of improvement within these roles promoting role satisfaction.

## II. GENERAL COMMENTS:

A role can be defined as a position that one holds in life which constitutes a portion of his/her self-image. Identity and satisfaction lie within how one feels within these roles. Attempts can be made to improve role satisfaction.

## III. POSSIBLE ACTIVITIES:

A. 1. Discuss new or challenging vocabulary.

   2. Prepare a game by cutting strips of paper and writing hypothetical roles on each, e.g., sister, brother, father, mother, worker, friend, student, volunteer, etc. Place in a "hat".

   3. Game proceeds as follows:
     a. Divide the class into two teams. Select two members at a time from each team to play "Password". Determine which team is to begin with a coin toss.
     b. Select a strip of paper from the "hat". Student #1 from both teams see the same strip of paper. They then try to convey the role to their teammate by using one word synonyms or words associated with the role. First clue = 10 points, second clue = 9 points, and so on until the role is correctly guessed or until the value of the clue = 1 point.
     c. If the role is not guessed, ask the class to guess, no points awarded.
     d. Continue round 2 with student #2 giving the clues and student #1 guessing. The team who correctly guessed the last role begins the next round.
     e. Select four new students for rounds 3 & 4, 5 & 6, etc. Play until a predetermined score (usually 25 points) is achieved or until time runs out.

   4. Reconvene as a class. Distribute handouts. Complete first section as a class activity.

   5. Instruct students to select one role and complete the handout, recalling vocabulary used during game to describe roles.

   6. Process need for role satisfaction.

B. 1. Encourage students to complete the handout.

   2. Collect work from students.

   3. Read from the handouts and encourage the class to guess the author.

   4. Process need for role satisfaction.

# Be your own best friend

*"Sometimes the best thing*

*you can do for yourself is reflect..."*

- When was the last time I truly felt good about myself? _____

_____

- What were the circumstances?

    setting (e.g., school/home/sports field/etc.) _____

    approximate age _____

    activity level _____

    family situation _____

    financial situation _____

    relationships/friendships _____

    grades _____

    self-image _____

    health _____

    weight _____

    physical fitness _____

    beliefs about self _____

    roles _____

    attitudes/emotions _____

    how my friends would have described me _____

- What can I do to restore any of these circumstances? _____

_____

- Therefore, my goal(s) is/are ... _____

_____

# Be your own best friend

I. PURPOSE:

To increase self-awareness by reflecting on positive past experiences.

To identify ways to restore those circumstances or create similar ones.

II. GENERAL COMMENTS:

In times of increased stress and/or depression, it may be difficult to remember when life was "better." It can be valuable to reflect on satisfying times, to identify and begin to restore some of the surrounding conditions.

III. POSSIBLE ACTIVITIES: This handout can be used in conjunction with GOAL SETTING PRACTICE SHEET (page 30) or GRIEF GRABS YOU (page 27).

A.  1. Discuss new or challenging vocabulary.

2. Distribute handout. Discuss concept of "best friends". List on chalkboard which qualities the class finds to be desirable in a best friend.

3. Discuss concept of "being your own best friend". Ask class to describe a person who is "being their own best friend." Compare and contrast the two lists. Use the lists to illustrate concept that "being your own best friend" and having a best friend will occur when all the qualities are self-recognized and self-realized.

4. Apply this technique in discussing relationships with members of the opposite sex.

5. Encourage members to complete handout.

6. Instruct each student to read their responses aloud. Encourage feedback and offer affirmations.

7. Discuss importance of past accomplishments, of recognizing that change is possible, and of the importance of setting goals to make positive changes.

B.  1. Distribute handouts. Instruct students to NOT write their name on handout. Discuss concept of "being your own best friend."

2. Encourage students to complete handout thoroughly.

3. Collect and shuffle.

4. Distribute them so that each student has one (not their own).

5. Give each student the opportunity to summarize the contents of the handout aloud and guess the author.

6. Continue until all students have had a turn.

7. Encourage feedback, affirmations and support.

8. Discuss importance of self-disclosure, recognizing past accomplishments, recognizing that change is possible, and the importance of setting goals to make positive changes.

# Influential people who have made an *imprint* on my life!

| | Influential people in my life. | What about them influenced/influences me? | How did/or does that influence my behavior? |
|---|---|---|---|
| **FAMILY MEMBERS** | | | |
| **FRIENDS** | | | |
| **TEACHERS** | | | |
| **PUBLIC FIGURES** | | | |
| **FICTIONAL CHARACTERS** | | | |
| **RELATIONSHIPS** | | | |
| **PEOPLE IN HISTORY** | | | |
| **CELEBRITIES** | | | |
| **CLERGY** | | | |
| **OTHER** | | | |

# Influential people who have made an *imprint* on my life!

I. PURPOSE:

To increase self-awareness by recognizing how people have influenced one's life.

II. GENERAL COMMENTS:

Many factors influence who we are today, e.g., education, money, values, religion, jobs, and **people**. This handout encourages one to look at the positive and/or negative influences people have had on his/her life.

III. POSSIBLE ACTIVITIES:

A. 1. Discuss new or challenging vocabulary.

2. Use the examples below to explain activity.

3. Encourage students to complete handout.

4. Facilitate discussion.

5. Process feelings experienced as a result of doing this activity.

|  | Influential people... | What about them... | How did/or... |
|---|---|---|---|
| Fictional characters | Wicked Witch of the West | she was evil and intentionally hurt people | allows me to be more sensitive to other people's fears. |
| Family | Grandfather | taking me to the circus | I love the circus and the memories it brings. |

B. 1. Write several examples of each category on separate index cards:

a. FAMILY MEMBERS (father, sister, aunt, grandfather)

b. PEOPLE IN HISTORY (J.F.K., Jonas Salk, Harriet Beecher Stowe)

2. Instruct students to choose one.

3. If this person has had an "imprint" on his/her life, he/she can share "what about them influenced me" and "how did or does that influence my behavior". If this person had no "imprint", the individual can pass the card to the right until someone can contribute or until the card goes back to the beginning. Encourage the next student to choose a new card, and the game continues.

4. Process feelings experienced as a result of doing this activity.

# Affirmations . . . which help me to be an **A+** me!

## PROGRESS

### PHYSICAL WELL-BEING
1. I _____
2. I _____

### SOCIAL WELL-BEING
1. I _____
2. I _____

### SCHOLASTIC WELL-BEING
1. I _____
2. I _____

## PROGRESS

### EMOTIONAL WELL-BEING
1. I _____
2. I _____

### FINANCIAL WELL-BEING
1. I _____
2. I _____

Grade ___A+___

Promoted to: _School of Positive Thinking_

Comments: _This promotion will last as long as you maintain this A+ attitude!_

_____
(Signature)

Affirmations...which help me to be

an $\mathbf{A}+$ me!

I.  PURPOSE:

To increase self-esteem by making positive affirmations.

II.  GENERAL COMMENTS:

Positive affirmations are self-esteem boosters!! There are several ways to state affirmations. Here is a list of some of them:
A.  I am . . .
B.  I can . . .
C.  I accept . . .
D.  I have . . .
E.  I feel . . .

III.  POSSIBLE ACTIVITIES:

A.  1.  Discuss new or challenging vocabulary.

   2.  Use the following examples (or your own) to illustrate the concept of the handout:

      a.  PHYSICAL WELL-BEING - I accept my body at it's present weight.

      b.  SOCIAL WELL-BEING - I have three very close friends who support me.

      c.  SCHOLASTIC WELL-BEING - I am capable of earning satisfactory grades.

      d.  EMOTIONAL WELL-BEING - I feel relaxed and in control of my life.

      e.  FINANCIAL WELL-BEING - I can learn to manage my money better by creating and living with a reasonable budget.

   3.  Instruct students to complete handout.

   4.  Encourage each student to share their complete list of affirmations.

   5.  Process importance of positive self-talk in regard to self-esteem.

B.  1.  Brainstorm with class possible items to include within each category of handout.

   2.  Instruct students to complete handout.

   3.  Prepare card game by labeling enough index cards for each student with each category listed on handout. Include a category labeled "OTHER AREAS OF WELL-BEING". Shuffle and place in a "hat".

   4.  Ask each student to choose a card and identify his/her affirmation within that category, ask them to extemporaneously create a new affirmation within that category.

   5.  Continue until all have shared and all cards have been discussed.

   6.  Process importance of positive self-talk in regard to self-esteem.

# I *will* like myself A to Z!

A. _____

B. _____

C. _____

D. _____

E. _____

F. _____

G. _____

h. _____

i. _____

J. _____

K. _____

L. _____

m. _____

n. _____

o. _____

P. _____

Q. _____

R. _____

S. _____

t. _____

U. _____

V. _____

W. _____

X. _exceptional_____

y. _____

Z. _____

I *will* like myself A to Z !

I. PURPOSE:

To increase self-esteem by acknowledging and accepting positive qualities regarding oneself.

II. GENERAL COMMENTS:

Positive affirmations can be created by using the alphabet as an outline. Acknowledging one's own positive qualities can be a powerful tool in boosting self-esteem.

III. POSSIBLE ACTIVITIES:

A. 1. Instruct each student to complete handout using the following format: ''I will like myself because I am . . .''

2. After each letter, a phrase or word beginning with that letter (or sound, if you like) should follow to complete the sentence, e.g.,
   R - receptive to new ideas
   X - exceptional at drawing cartoons

3. Process benefits of positive affirmations and impact on self-esteem.

B. 1. Distribute the handouts and ask each student to put his/her name at the top of the page.

2 Collect and redistribute handouts so that everyone has someone else's paper.

3. Instruct students to insert one adjective or phrase after one letter of the alphabet, describing something positive about that student.

4. Encourage each student to put one positive comment on each of his classmates' handouts, continuing to pass them around until 26 comments are on each and all are returned.

5. Invite each student to read his/her handout aloud to the class. Applaud efforts.

6. Process benefits of positive affirmations and impact on self-esteem.

# Certificate

*In recognition of your efforts and accomplishments in the following area(s):*

_____

_____

_____

(name)

_____

(school)

*is awarded this certificate at*

*Congratulations!*

_____

(date)

*Certificate*

I.  PURPOSE:

To increase self-esteem by recognizing efforts and accomplishments.

II.  GENERAL COMMENTS:

It is easy to allow noteworthy efforts and accomplishments to go unrecognized. With this handout, these events can be written and displayed to serve as a visual reminder of success.

III.  POSSIBLE ACTIVITIES:

A.  Complete this handout to recognize . . .

1.  Completion of a class, lecture, goal, project, other activity.

2.  Increased skill level (assertion, time management, stress management).

3.  Attendance.

4.  Other noteworthy efforts and accomplishments.

B.  1.  Ask one student to temporarily leave the room.

2.  While s/he is out, ask the other students to decide which positive areas to recognize in the student at that particular time.

3.  Allow student to rejoin class, be presented with the certificate, receive standing ovation and applause.

4.  Proceed with all students.

5.  Process benefits of this activity.

# Self-Esteem

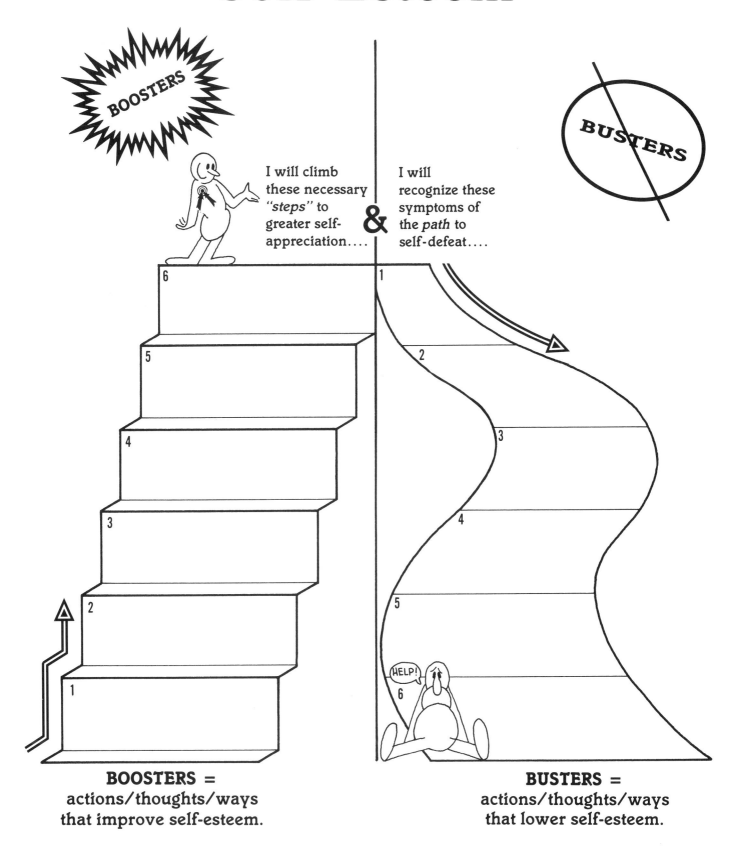

# Self-Esteem

I.  PURPOSE:

To increase self-esteem by creating *steps* to greater self-appreciation and recognizing symptoms of self-defeat.

II. GENERAL COMMENTS:

Self-esteem boosters are positive *steps* one can take to lead to greater self-appreciation. Self-esteem busters are negative influences that lead to self-defeat.

III. POSSIBLE ACTIVITIES:

A.  1. Discuss new or challenging vocabulary.

2. Explain concept by giving example of a celebrity:
   a.) Instruct the class to list the options and opportunities this celebrity has to "boost" his/her self-esteem.
   b.) Instruct the class to list the events that could occur to "bust" his/her self-esteem.

3. Instruct the class to complete the handout listing their own busters and boosters.

4. Collect and read each aloud with others guessing the author of each.

5. Process benefits of this activity.

B.  1. Facilitate brainstorming on chalkboard regarding ideas for each category.

2. Encourage discussion regarding impact of self-esteem busters and boosters on wellness.

3. Instruct the class to complete the handout listing their own busters and boosters.

4. Process benefits of this activity.

I ♥ Me

## I. PURPOSE:

To identify positive, personal characteristics.

To increase self-esteem by receiving sincere compliments and positive feedback from others.

## II. GENERAL COMMENTS:

Identifying positive characteristics one possesses and accepting positive feedback from others, can contribute to a healthy self-image and increase self-esteem. Focusing on one's strengths rather than weaknesses, will ultimately enhance performance in daily activities and improve relationships.

## III. POSSIBLE ACTIVITIES:

A. 1. Introduce topics of self-image and self-esteem, with definitions from students and teacher's input as needed. Discuss new or challenging vocabulary.

2. Distribute handouts and instruct each student to write his/her name on the "collar" of the "I Love Me" shirt.

3. Instruct students to pass papers to the student next to them or behind them, so that each student can write or draw 2 positive comments on each other's shirt (not in the heart-shaped space).

4. When each student receives his/her own T-shirt, s/he is to write 5-10 positive comments in the heart-shaped space.

5. Share as a class activity, asking each student to stand and read all comments on T-shirt. Compare and contrast class comments vs. student's own comments.

6. Give applause after each student reads his/hers aloud.

7. Process benefits of this activity.

B. 1. Introduce topics of self-image and self-esteem, with definition from students and teacher's input as needed.

2. Use this handout as a "good-bye" activity for a student who might be leaving or at the closing session of the SEALS Program.

3. Ask each student who is leaving or completing the SEALS program, to have a "good-bye conversation" with the teacher in a separate room or in a quiet corner of the classroom for approximately 10 minutes. At the same time, the class completes the "I Love Me" handout by passing the paper around the class, so that each student has an opportunity to write or draw 2 positive comments about the person who is leaving.

4. Invite the student to rejoin the class when completed.

5. Pass the same paper around the class and ask each student to read aloud the comments that s/he wrote.

6. Provide an opportunity for the student who is leaving to reflect on his/her thoughts and feelings of the activity, including identifying his/her favorite comments.

7. Process benefits of giving and receiving compliments and how this affects self-image and self-esteem.

# Make "Sense" of your ...
## SELF - IMAGE

| | SEE | HEAR | TASTE | SMELL | TOUCH |
|---|---|---|---|---|---|
| **S** | | | | | |
| **E** | | | | | |
| **L** | | | | | |
| **F** | | | | | |
| **I** | | | | | |
| **M** | | | | | |
| **A** | | | | | |
| **G** | | | | | |
| **E** | | | | | |

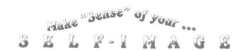

Make "Sense" of your ...
# SELF-IMAGE

I. PURPOSE:

To identify various components that contribute to self-image.

To identify ways to self-nurture with appeal to the 5 senses.

II. GENERAL COMMENTS:

Self-image is how one "sees" or views oneself, and is affected by many factors. It can be influenced in a positive way when one is nurtured with enjoyable activities, experiences, and surroundings.

III. POSSIBLE ACTIVITIES:

A. 1. Compile kit of sense-stimulators and how it relates to self-nurturance.

e.g., SEE - landscape photographs, travel brochures, clear container of sand, plants, pictures of a party, people laughing, restaurant, sunset, video games, books and magazines.

HEAR - tapes of different kinds of music, environmental sounds, sound effects, pictures of electronic equipment cut from advertisements or catalogs, relaxation tapes, radio/record player/tape player etc.

TASTE - cookies, fresh vegetables, fresh fruit, beverages (or illustrations).

SMELL - spices, potpourri, aftershave/perfume, flowers, lemon.

TOUCH - satin, silk, cotton, animal fur, wool, burlap, corrugated paper.

2. Introduce concept of self-image and how it relates to self-nurturance.

3. Discuss new or challenging vocabulary.

4. Distribute handouts.

5. Introduce the sense of sight by encouraging students to experience each sight-stimulator from the kit.

6. Instruct students to jot down (in the SEE column) either the sense-stimulator from the kit or their own ideas, which they find to be self-nurturing.

7. Discuss and share as able.

8. Proceed with sense of hearing, sense of taste, sense of smell, and the sense of touch, as explained above in A. 5-7.

9. Process benefits of self-nurturance in conjunction with these five senses.

B. 1. Introduce concept of self-image and how it relates to self-nurturance.

2. Distribute handouts and explain as follows:

a. In each block, students are to write **any** activity, experience or surrounding which appeals to that particular sense and begins with the corrensponding letter in the word "self-image". For example, using the letter **E**; SEE - **e**ntertainers

HEAR - **e**xcellent jokes

TASTE - **e**ating pizza

SMELL - **e**arly morning breakfast

TOUCH - **e**njoying hugs

b. When grid is complete, highlight those activities that are not presently incorporated into the student's lifestyle, but could be considered for the future.

3. Share responses as a class, setting goals as appropriate.

4. Process concept of self-image and how it relates to self-nurturance.

**Are you "under" STRESS?**

## STRESS SYMPTOMS

**I know I'm under stress when I...(✓)**

- ☐ Cry more than usual
- ☐ Can't sleep
- ☐ Eat more than usual
- ☐ Am irritable
- ☐ Resort to the use of alcohol/drugs
- ☐ Have "physical complaints"
- ☐ Bite fingernails

- ☐ Experience skin problems
- ☐ Have difficulty concentrating/focusing
- ☐ Sleep more than usual
- ☐ Don't feel like eating
- ☐ Am on the move all the time—fidgety
- ☐ Become overly sensitive
- ☐ Don't feel like doing anything
- ☐ Other _____

## STRESS REDUCERS

**When I see these "symptoms," I will...( ✓ and be specific)**

- ☐ Go for a walk _____ for _____ mins.
- ☐ Read a good book _____ for _____ mins.
- ☐ Go shopping at _____ for _____ mins.
- ☐ Exercise _____ for _____ mins.
- ☐ Listen to music on the _____
- ☐ Write in my journal _____
- ☐ Use relaxation techniques _____
- ☐ Take some time for myself by _____
- ☐ Do something I'm skilled at _____ for _____ mins.
- ☐ Talk to my friend, counselor, teacher, family member, someone else _____
- ☐ Say "No" to _____
- ☐ Confront the situation by _____
- ☐ Limit certain behaviors _____
- ☐ List my responsibilities in order of importance # 1 _____

  # 2 _____

  # 3 _____

- ☐ Other _____

**Are you
"under"
STRESS?**

I.  PURPOSE:

To increase awareness of stress symptoms and reducers, promoting effective management of stress.

II.  GENERAL COMMENTS:

People are often unaware of their stress symptoms. An active approach to stress management includes recognizing stress symptoms and pairing them with specific stress reducers. In this manner, one can develop new coping skill patterns.

III.  POSSIBLE ACTIVITIES:

A.  1.  Discuss new or challenging vocabulary.

2.  Distribute handouts to class and allow them to have 60 seconds to look at the handout, remembering as much as they can.

3.  After turning over the handouts, encourage class to recall as much as they can as one student writes on the chalkboard under two categories: symptoms and coping skills.

4.  Complete the chalkboard list by referring to the handout, and facilitate discussion encouraging students to add to the list.

5.  Instruct students to complete handout.

6.  Process benefits of coping with stress.

B.  1.  Explain that stress symptoms "creep up" slowly and with no "announcement".

2.  Instruct class to complete handout.

3.  Divide class into small groups of three to share responses.

4.  After a specified time, encourage students to reconvene and process the benefits of coping with stress.

ANNOYANCES  STRESS  IRRITANTS  HASSLES
PEEVES  ANNOYANCES
HASSLES  STRESS
IRRITANTS  PEEVES

# Don't sweat the "SMALL STUFF"

- Stressors come in all sizes and all forms . . .
  some are major life events . . .
  but MANY are everyday hassles . . .
  or . . . "small stuff".
- Effective coping skills can help to put these in perspective.

| HASSLE / EXPERIENCE | MY REACTION | POSSIBLE COPING SKILLS |
|---|---|---|
| 1. | | |
| 2. | | |
| 3. | | |

Don't sweat the
"SMALL STUFF"

I. PURPOSE:

To recognize the difference between major life stressors, and everyday hassles that create stress.

To develop an awareness of typical reactions to everyday hassles and identify more effective means to cope.

II. GENERAL COMMENTS:

Stress can come in all sizes and, if mismanaged, can have an unhealthy impact. Learning to gain control over the "small stuff" can contribute greatly to one's sense of wellness.

III. POSSIBLE ACTIVITIES:

A. 1. Discuss new or challenging vocabulary.

2. Generate discussion of varying degrees of stress, including students' examples of major life stressors, as well as everyday hassles/annoyances/peeves/irritants.

3. Discuss sources of stress, attempting to focus stress management in one category per students' interests and needs,
      e.g.,  family,
            school,
            finances,
            time issues,
            self-talk,
            relationships, etc.

4. Decide on one category as a focus for this SEALS session. Use one example from the class on the chalkboard,
      e.g.,  FAMILY

| HASSLE/EXPERIENCE | MY REACTION | POSSIBLE COPING SKILLS |
|---|---|---|
| Sibling is always borrowing my things without permission. | resentment anger hostility | assertiveness _____ asking parents for help |

5. Distribute handout, asking students to complete handout with chosen category.

6. Pursue discussion of possible coping skills within that category.

7. Process benefits of this activity.

8. Choose additional categories for future SEALS sessions.

B. 1. Generate discussion of varying degrees of stress, including students' examples of major life stressors, as well as everyday hassles/annoyances/peeves/irritants.

2. Distribute handout and instruct class to complete.

3. Formulate a list of "possible coping skills" on the chalkboard from all students' responses. Add others as able.

4. Discuss wide range of options in coping with "small stuff".

5. Process benefits of this activity.

# HOW I'M GOING TO MAKE
## STRESS
### WORK FOR ME !

STRESS

Name _____

#1    When I see that I _____
                                                    Stress Symptom(s)
      I will _____

      _____

#2    When I see that I _____
                                                    Stress Symptom(s)
      I will _____

      _____

#3    When I see that I _____
                                                    Stress Symptom(s)
      I will _____

      _____

#4    When I see that I _____
                                                    Stress Symptom(s)
      I will _____

      _____

#5    When I see that I _____
                                                    Stress Symptom(s)
      I will _____

      _____

# HOW I'M GOING TO MAKE
## STRESS
### WORK FOR ME !

I. PURPOSE:

To improve stress management by use of the self-contract method.

II. GENERAL COMMENTS:

Being able to identify stress symptoms and pair them with specific stress reducers is a powerful way to change behavior and increase self-management.

III. POSSIBLE ACTIVITIES:

A.  1. Discuss new or challenging vocabulary.

 2. Elicit possible stress symptoms from students and list them on the left side of the chalkboard.

 3. Elicit stress reducers and write them on the right side of the chalkboard.

 4. Encourage students to see if any of them could be paired, and items on the 2 lists can then be used as effective self-contracting goals.

 5. Instruct class to complete handout with goals for relieving their own stress symptoms.

 6. Process importance of stress management and impact of self-contracts.

B.  1. Use this handout in conjunction with ARE YOU UNDER STRESS? (page 58). Instruct students to create goals from their checked boxes.

 2. Encourage students to read their completed self-contract for the entire class and seek feedback.

 3. Process importance of stress management and impact of self-contracts.

# DO ANY OF THESE STRESSORS "HIT HOME"?

*Day-to-day life has countless stressors. Identifying even the smallest irritant, as well as major life stressors, assists us in recognizing the amount of stress we actually encounter... and the VALUE of coping skills.*

*Stressors can have an increased effect and unhealthy results relating to personal well being, relationships, and other life areas.*

*Check (✔) below the stressors you've experienced in the last few months.*

☐ Your alarm clock not going off.
☐ Your favorite sports team losing.
☐ A recent illness.
☐ Hearing gossip about a close friend.
☐ Parents/relatives getting a divorce.
☐ Losing a friend's long-distance phone number.
☐ Working on a project with unorganized people.
☐ Not being able to find a kleenex... and needing it!
☐ Birth of a new brother/sister.
☐ Being late on a deadline.
☐ Harassing phone calls.
☐ Ending a relationship.
☐ Parent under stress.
☐ Recent death of someone close to you.
☐ Having difficulty motivating yourself.
☐ Losing a game.
☐ Wanting to eat, but on a diet.
☐ Having only cold water for a bath.
☐ Friends not calling.
☐ Not being able to find keys.
☐ Waiting for progress report/report card.
☐ Failing a test.
☐ Someone telling you what to do.
☐ Moving to a new city.
☐ Not enough time for yourself.
☐ Forgetting birthday of someone important to you.
☐ Forgetting lunch money.
☐ Threat of war.
☐ Planning a large event.
☐ Friends pressuring you to drink alcohol/use
    drugs/do something you really don't want to do.

☐ Anniversary of a loved one's death.
☐ Not having enough money.
☐ Parents treating you like a little child.
☐ A new school.
☐ Someone telling you how to feel.
☐ Having trouble understanding difficult subject.
☐ Having no money and not wanting to borrow.
☐ Arguing with a good friend or relative.
☐ Out-of-town relatives staying with you.
☐ Friends being too dependent on you.
☐ Lack of privacy.
☐ Parents putting pressure on you.
☐ Not feeling well and not knowing why.
☐ Best friend asking to borrow money.
☐ An appliance/machine not working.
☐ Too much to do, not enough time.
☐ Someone canceling plans one-half hour before.
☐ Moving to a new house or apartment.
☐ Good friend feeling depressed.
☐ Being late for the school bus/ride to school.
☐ Losing a valuable possession/important paper.
☐ Forgetting locker combination.
☐ Saying "yes" to too many things.
☐ Waiting in a long line.
☐ Being charged too much money.
☐ Electricity going out.
☐ Auditions/tryouts.
☐ College entrance exams.
☐ Being in trouble with the law/school/teachers.
☐ _____
☐ _____

*These stressors may not change, however your ability to "cope" with them CAN change!*

# STRESSORS "HIT HOME"?

I. PURPOSE:

To identify stressors as a first step in stress management.

II. GENERAL COMMENTS:

Common stressors are often overlooked and left unidentified. Without identifying them, it is impossible to recognize the need for stress management.

III. POSSIBLE ACTIVITIES:

A. 1. Discuss new or challenging vocabulary.

2. Facilitate discussion of stressors by brainstorming a list of irritants on chalkboard.

3. Distribute handouts. Ask students to skim handout to compare and contrast their list on chalkboard with information listed on handout.

4. Instruct students to complete handout.

5. Ask students to total checked boxes to compare numbers. Ask class to analyze significance of results, i.e., What does it mean if the majority of students scored over 40, 35, etc.?

6. Encourage class to discuss stress management techniques they have/can develop.

7. Process importance of recognizing potential stressors and ways to cope with them.

B. 1. Facilitate discussion of identifying stressors as a first step in stress management.

2. Distribute handouts and instruct students to complete.

3. Review areas checked. Ask students which stressors they were surprised to see, or were unaware of, that contributed to their stress level. Discuss.

4. Encourage students to discuss stress management techniques they have/plan to develop.

5. Process importance of recognizing potential stressors and ways to cope with them.

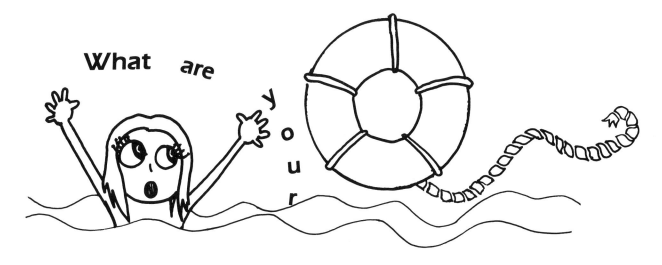

# "LIFESAVERS"?    Who? Where? How?

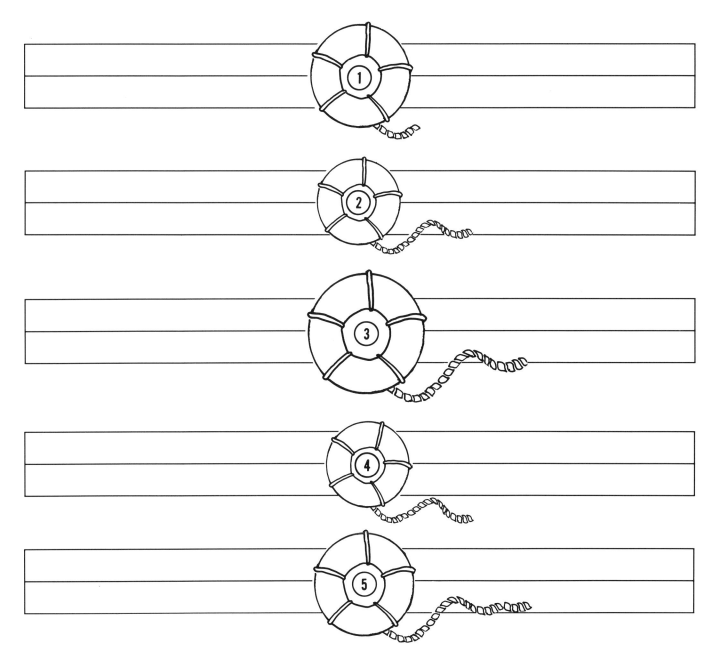

# "LIFESAVERS"?

## I. PURPOSE:

To identify various means of support.

To establish a plan to utilize designated support systems more effectively.

## II. GENERAL COMMENTS:

Support systems are vital to an individual's well-being, however often are not established or utilized effectively. Individuals can increase their independence by knowing when and how to utilize these supports.

## III. POSSIBLE ACTIVITIES:

A.  1. Discuss new or challenging vocabulary.

2. Ask class for a definition of lifesaver and inquire how this relates to wellness.

3. Ask class to brainstorm on the board this situation:

A student has had a difficult and challenging day. S/he is drained physically and mentally. S/he has a long and complicated assignment to complete for homework along with household chores. What can s/he do? What would be a lifesaver?

| "LIFESAVERS" | Who? Where? How? |
| --- | --- |
| a good listener | father, friend, neighbor |
| exercise | take dog for a walk |

4. Distribute handouts and encourage students to complete.

5. Share responses as a class activity focusing on goal setting (see Unit 6) and coping behaviors (see Unit 4).

6. Close by processing benefits of this activity through different situations in the students' lives, e.g., lifesavers at school, home, with friends, babysitting, on the school bus, etc.

B.  1. Introduce topic of support systems.

2. Distribute 3 handouts to each student.

3. Decide, as a class, different categories of needs, e.g., physical, emotional, spiritual, school, social, work-related, personal.

4. Select one category from the list and brainstorm on chalkboard possible lifesavers.

e.g.,   PHYSICAL-Someone is feeling a lack of energy.

| "LIFESAVERS" | Who? Where? How? |
| --- | --- |
| getting enough sleep | going to bed earlier |
| taking breaks | going outside for lunch |
| crying | giving myself permission to cry in front of friends |
| exercising | going for a walk, horseback riding |
| eating fresh fruits/vegetables | go to the health food store |

5. Continue by asking the class to select 3 categories from the list on the chalkboard. Facilitate a discussion of these 3 categories where a situation might arise that would require a lifesaver.

6. Encourage class to complete their three handouts.

7. Ask students to share possible answers.

8. Process benefits of identifying various means of support.

# NO ONE is an
# "Iₛ-LAND"

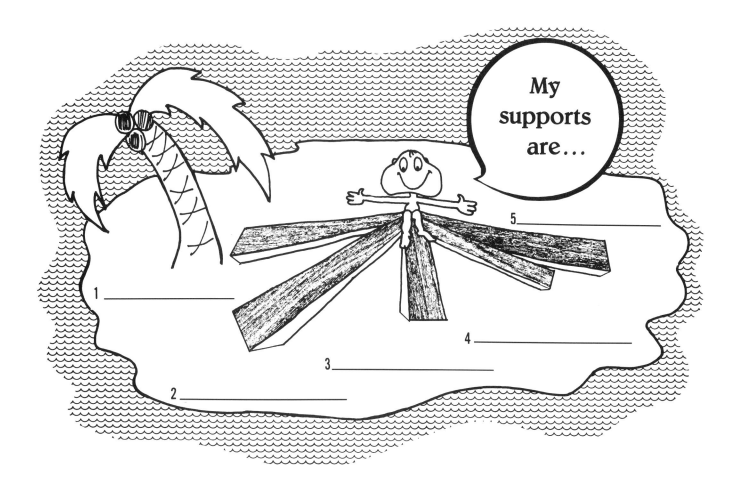

- One valuable "SURVIVAL SKILL" is having supports in our lives to help us cope.

- Fill in the names of your "SUPPORTS" above.

- If you were not able to fill in all 5, how or where can you find them?

_____

_____

_____

_____

**NO ONE is an**

# "Is-LAND"

## I. PURPOSE:

To identify present support systems and possible need for additional ones.

To identify ways to increase support systems.

## II. GENERAL COMMENTS:

It is important to have at least five supports at any given time in one's life. A network including individuals, groups, pets, organizations, family, friends, etc., allows for a more effective means of support.

## III. POSSIBLE ACTIVITIES:

A. 1. Discuss new or challenging vocabulary.

2. Become familiarized with the novel Robinson Crusoe by Daniel Defoe or use any short story or novel with which the class might be familiar.

3. Distribute handout. Use illustration to facilitate discussion of support systems. Facilitate discussion using the novel or short story and the main characters' support system.

4. Encourage students to brainstorm possible personal support systems on chalkboard, e.g., school, home, social, medical, church, recreation.

5. Ask students to consider these areas of support while completing the top half of the handout.

6. Encourage class to share their identified supports with entire class.

7. Ask the class to imagine that these supports were not available at the time. Instruct class to complete the bottom half of the handout. Seek feedback from the class regarding how / where to increase number of supports as needed.

8. Process benefits of support systems in regards to wellness.

B. 1. Explain concept of support systems.

2. Encourage student to complete handout first. Then, on the back of the handout, ask them to create a list of why each of these supports are helpful to them.

3. Give each student an opportunity to share his/her list of supports and why they are helpful.

4. Process by encouraging student to identify something s / he learned from this activity.

| NAME: | TYPE OF SERVICE: | ADDRESS: | PHONE #: |
|---|---|---|---|
| 1 | | | |
| | | | |
| | | | |
| | | | |
| 2 | | | |
| | | | |
| | | | |
| | | | |
| 3 | | | |
| | | | |
| | | | |
| | | | |
| 4 | | | |
| | | | |
| | | | |
| | | | |
| 5 | | | |
| | | | |
| | | | |
| | | | |

# There ARE community resources !

## I. PURPOSE:

To increase awareness of community resources which may act to increase one's support system.

## II. GENERAL COMMENTS:

Community resources are available, but often people are unaware of them. By educating individuals about possible community resources and encouraging them to list the most applicable, this handout can then be a visual reminder and assist with follow-through.

## III. POSSIBLE ACTIVITIES:

A.  1. Discuss new or challenging vocabulary.

2. Assemble several sets of current telephone directories. Consider the consumer (Yellow Pages) phone book, toll-free 800 numbers directory, federal, state, county or community directories. Also, local or state-wide school systems, wellness or health network directories might be available. Check your library for almanacs, directories of organizations and associations, or The Address Book, and Who's Who. (There are many specialized editions such as Who's Who in Education or Who's Who in Support Services.)

3. Distribute handouts. Recall prior discussion (see page 62) of categories of needs, and list on chalkboard.

4. Divide the class into small groups. Give each group a set of directories.

5. Refresh their knowledge of using the index and proper subject headings in order to successfully use a telephone directory.

6. Instruct each group to use their directories to locate the names, addresses and phone numbers of resources available to them in each category of need listed on the chalkboard.

7. Reconvene as a class and ask one representative from each group to share from their list.

8. Facilitate:
   a.) a discussion of telephone etiquette. Role-play using potential resources to practice phone-calling skills.
   b.) a discussion of letter-writing techniques.

9. Ask the class to make one phone call or write a letter to one resource on their lists before the next session. Inform them that they will be asked to share the results/outcome of their call or letter during the next SEALS session.

10. Close with a discussion of the availability and importance of community resources.

B.  1. Before the class, use telephone directories to locate and list the name, address and phone numbers of 40-50 possible community resources on index cards. (This can be assigned to a group of students. Ask them for their assistance before school, during lunch or during a free period.)

2. Locate information in several categories, e.g., religious, educational, volunteer, emotional support, social, recreational, etc.

3. Distribute handouts to class.

4. Ask each student, in turn, to select one card and read it aloud, discussing the resource and services available.

5. Instruct students, who are interested in this resource, to write it on their handout.

6. Proceed until all students have had a turn and five resources are listed on each sheet.

7. Close with discussion of support networks and process benefits of doing this activity.

# Are you on "BRAIN OVERLOAD"?

Do you feel like you have a "*million*" things to get done . . . RIGHT NOW?

1st  Step — Write them down

2nd Step — Indicate #1 — if this is the "*best*" use of your time RIGHT NOW.
Indicate #2 — if this is a "*good*" use of your time RIGHT NOW.
Indicate #3 — if this is a "*waste*" of your time RIGHT NOW.

3rd  Step — Insert all of your #1's in the "*Today*" list on page 2.
Insert all of your #2's in the "*Next Few Days*" list on page 2.
Insert all of your #3's in the "*Waste of my time right now*!" list on page 2.

A _____ = # _____

B _____ = # _____

C _____ = # _____

D _____ = # _____

E _____ = # _____

F _____ = # _____

G _____ = # _____

H _____ = # _____

I _____ = # _____

J _____ = # _____

*(continued on page 2)*

**Are you on**

## "BRAIN OVERLOAD"?

I.  PURPOSE:

To improve time management skills by prioritizing tasks.

II.  GENERAL COMMENTS:

"Brain Overload" refers to the overwhelming feeling that occurs when there are an increasing number of pressures and responsibilities to be addressed. Ineffective time management can be a stressor.

III.  POSSIBLE ACTIVITIES:

A.  1.  Discuss new or challenging vocabulary.

2.  Distribute handouts. Use illustration and definition of "Brain Overload" to facilitate discussion.

3.  Encourage class to use the handout to list all the things that they have to get done RIGHT NOW. Create a simulated atmosphere of pressure by walking around, reading over their shoulders, talking loudly, causing distractions, putting a time limit on the assignment and reminding them often of the amount of time remaining.

4.  Ask the class for feedback on their emotions, stress level and quality of work in a high pressure situation.

5.  Allow them additional time to review and complete their list in a more relaxed atmosphere.

6.  Reviewing the directions, instruct the class to complete the 2nd step of the activity as indicated. Possible examples ....

a.  clean closet       =    #3

b.  complete homework =   #1

c.  mowing lawn       =    #2

7.  Distribute "BRAIN OVERLOAD" handout (Page 65).

8.  Instruct the class to complete the 3rd step of the activity, listing all #1 activities from page 64 in the TODAY section, #2 activities in the NEXT FEW DAYS section and #3's in WASTE OF MY TIME RIGHT NOW section.

9.  Facilitate discussion by asking students to share their top priorities with the class, encouraging feedback from others.

10.  Close with discussion of insights gained from doing this activity.

B.  1.  Begin with a discussion regarding the importance of prioritizing to decrease stress/increase success.

2.  Encourage students to cite:
a.) times when they have allowed tasks to get out of control and create stress.
b.) times in their lives when effective time management increased their sense of success.

3.  Explain system utilized in handout.

4.  Instruct students to complete both handouts.

5.  Facilitate discussion by asking students to share top priorities, encouraging feedback from others.

6.  Process benefits of this activity.

# Brain Overload?

**#1**                                    **Today**

_____
_____
_____
_____
_____


**#2**                                **Next Few Days**

_____
_____
_____
_____
_____


**#3**                          **Waste of my time right now!**

_____
_____
_____
_____
_____

## BRAIN OVERLOAD ?

I. PURPOSE:

To improve time management skills by placing tasks into three time slots for completion.

II. GENERAL COMMENTS:

This handout can be used in conjunction with ARE YOU ON BRAIN OVERLOAD? (page 65), or individually as a visual reminder and an organizational tool.

III. POSSIBLE ACTIVITIES:

A.  1. Instruct students to complete this handout after finishing ARE YOU ON BRAIN OVERLOAD? (page 65).

2. Process resultant feelings of organizing tasks into time slots.

B.  1. Distribute packet of seven handouts to each student.

2. Instruct students to write their names and the next seven dates on each page. Inform the class that this activity will require follow-up in one week. To prepare for the day ahead, the class is to complete one form every morning for the next seven days. Preferably, the handout should be completed at home each day before departure for school, but can be completed in school if time and schedule allows.

3. Collect finished packets after one week.

4. Select one packet at a time and read top priorities aloud and elicit feedback from class.

5. Close with discussion of possible benefits of this activity.

# TIME for TIPS & TIPS for TIME

**Review the following list and choose the tips that fit your particular time management needs!**
**Remember to make a time management plan of your own so that it fits your personality.**
**This way, it will work better for you!!!**

1. Set realistic goals.
_____

2. Make a list of tasks. Write the most important ones first, less important second, and so on.
_____

3. Give yourself permission to say "NO".
_____

4. Know what time of the day is best for you and plan activities around these times.
_____

5. Ask yourself "What's the best use of my time right now?" and focus on that particular activity.
_____

6. Remind yourself how good it feels to finish a task.
_____

7. Ask others for help.
_____

8. Make a decision quickly and stick to it.
_____

9. Keep a positive attitude when faced with a difficult task. Break it down into smaller, easier steps.
_____

10. Make use of "waiting" time, by having small, tasks/activities to do...or simply plan to enjoy this time and relax.
_____

11. Ask for a quiet time or a quiet place. Create a place where you can work comfortably and without interruptions.
_____

12. Reward yourself.
_____

13. Remember...you don't have to be perfect.
_____

14. Free time, leisure time, and exercise are important too.
_____

**Circle three "tips for time" that you can incorporate into your individualized time management system:**

1    2    3    4    5    6    7    8    9    10    11    12    13    14

**GOAL Write one goal which needs attention now:** _____

_____

*A balanced lifestyle is a positive outcome of effective time management.*

I.  PURPOSE:

To identify components for an individualized time management system.

To establish one immediate time management goal.

II.  GENERAL COMMENTS:

Effective time management is beneficial to self-esteem, relationships with others, life balance, and most all other aspects of life. By evaluating various time management tips, one can design an effective, individualized time management system.

III.  POSSIBLE ACTIVITIES: This handout can be used in conjunction with TIME MYTHOLOGY (page 68).

A.  1.  Discuss new or challenging vocabulary.

2.  Distribute handouts and discuss time management tips.

3.  Distribute a blank card to each student.

4.  Instruct them to write a time management tip s/he would like to share with the group, e.g., writing homework in an assignment notebook.

5.  Collect cards and put in a basket.

6.  Pass basket around and instruct students to choose one card (not their own) and read aloud. Encourage discussion of each tip.

7.  Compare and contrast the time management tips from the class with those on the handout.

8.  Close by asking each student to name one time management tip they plan to use.

B.  1.  Distribute handout and discuss time management tips.

2.  Encourage students to write in the spaces provided, comments to assist them with their own personal situations.

3.  Elicit feedback from the class on additional time management tips.

4.  Instruct members to set appropriate goals.

5.  Process benefits of effective time management.

6.  Close by asking each student to name one time management tip they plan to use.

# TIME MYTHOLOGY

Each of us has the same amount of time in each day, week, month, and year. What we have been taught about time, and how well we organize and spend our time, can differ greatly among us.

Below are some typical TIME-MYTHS, that can lead to poor time management. Re-write each TIME-MYTH making a REALITY-STATEMENT. The first one has been done for you.

THE PURPOSE: To help you find out what's *real* and *not real* about time, and to help you manage your time with greater success.

| TIME-MYTHS | REALITY-STATEMENTS |
|---|---|
| *"If I only had 2 more hours in each day, I'd be able to get it done."* | I have 24 hours just like everyone else. I need to list priorities and have a realistic schedule. |
| *"Time management is boring; it doesn't work for me."* | |
| *"I need someone else to motivate me or I won't get it done."* | |
| *"I'm waiting until I have more time."* | |
| *"People keep interrupting me, so I can't get anything done."* | |
| *"They have so much more time than I do."* | |
| | |

## Taking more control of your time, allows you more control of your life!

# TIMƩ MYTHOLOGY

## I. PURPOSE:

To increase time management by recognizing typical unproductive, unreasonable, and/or overstated thoughts associated with time.

To increase time management by identifying *reality-statements* to offset typical *time-myths*.

## II. GENERAL COMMENTS:

Frequently, *time-myths* hinder time management skills. These thoughts border on being irrational, and need to be put in perspective. *Reality-statements* provide a more rational approach to hopefully assist in managing time more effectively.

## III. POSSIBLE ACTIVITIES: This handout can be used in conjunction with TIME FOR TIPS & TIPS FOR TIME (page 67).

A.  1. Discuss new and challenging vocabulary.

2. Introduce topic with definition of a myth and famous myths that the class can recall. Remind them that most ancient cultures had powerful myths that people believed and which controlled many aspects of their lives.

3. Ask the class to discuss any myths or folktales that our culture might hold.

4. Present the concept of time-myths and their effect on time management.

5. Distribute handouts and review. Offer the 5 listed time-myths as examples of typical thoughts associated with time. Discuss which communication style would choose to accept the time-myths, reviewing pages 7-8 if necessary.

6. Encourage class to add others in appropriate spaces. Brainstorm on chalkboard as needed.

7. Instruct the class to re-write the time-myths, using the example on the handout or thoughts of your own.

8. Ask students to share their statements, encouraging feedback from the class.

9. Discuss possible benefits of this activity.

10. Close by discussing last statement on handout.

B.  1. Facilitate a discussion of the concept of time-myths and their effects on time management by reading aloud the three sentences under illustration.

2. Distribute blank sheets of paper and pencils to the class.

3. Read aloud each time-myth, #1-10, asking class to respond to the question:
    "When do you hear yourself saying this, or thinking this?"

Ask group members to write down their responses, trying to answer each one differently,
    e.g., Time-Myth  #1-when I am late in calling friends back.
                     #2-whenever the topic of exercise comes up.
                     #3-when I need more leisure time.
                     #4-when I see time management books in the library.
                     #5-when friends ask me to go out.
                     #6-when drawing or sketching.
                     #7-when household chores are waiting for me.
                     #8-when I'm doing homework.
                     #9-when I look at my friends' lifestyles.
                     #10-at nighttime when I'm going over the day's activities.

4. Distribute handouts, instructing class to complete by filling in their *reality-statements*.

5. Process benefits of this activity.

6. Close with a discussion of the last statement on handout.

# BALANCE

## YOUR

**L**EISURE
**I**NDIVIDUAL CARE
**F**REE / UNSCHEDULED TIME
**E**FFORTS IN SCHOOL/WORK ACTIVITIES

## I. PURPOSE:

To increase awareness of how much time is spent daily in the 4 life areas: leisure, individual care, free/unscheduled time, and efforts in school/work activities.

To acknowledge changes needed for improved life balance.

To identify a plan which provides a healthy daily balance among these 4 life areas.

## II. GENERAL COMMENTS:

Wellness can be defined in terms of an adequate life balance (leisure, individual care, free/unscheduled time, and efforts in school/work activities). Life balance contributes to a healthy self-concept and to an individual's ability to cope with stress. There is not a set amount of time that is recommended for each life area. However, individuals need to determine and control their own healthy balance of activities. Identifying how time is spent on a daily basis allows accurate analysis of strengths/weaknesses in one's scheduling.

## III. POSSIBLE ACTIVITIES:

A. 1. Before class, you will need to empty four eggshells. To do this, make a small hole in the wider end of the egg, and remove the contents. Also you will need a small pair of scissors, masking tape, and some books, all about the same size. (Do not remove the egg from the shell the traditional way by making two holes on each end of the eggshell and forcing the contents out of the shell by blowing it out. The holes will weaken the structure of the shell and defeat the purpose of the demonstration.)

2. Put a piece of masking tape around the middle of each eggshell. This will prevent the eggshell from cracking when you cut it.

3. Carefully cut around the eggshell through the masking tape, so that you have four eggshell halves with even bottoms.

4. Place the eggshells on a table or desk, dome side up, in a rectangle that's just a bit smaller than one of the books.

5. Ask a volunteer to guess how many books it would take to break the eggshells.

6. Select one student to put books on the eggshells until the eggshells crack or break. Compare the class estimate with the actual number.

7. Ask the class to determine why the eggshells could withstand a great amount of stress from the books. (Structure of the shell is stronger lengthwise and the stress of the weight of the books is distributed by the dome shape of the shell.)

8. Use the demonstration to facilitate discussion of life balance and relationship to one's own stress level and self-concept. Each eggshell could be used to represent one life area and that with balance, reinforcement, and coping skills, "cracking" under stress can be avoided or prevented.

9. Distribute handouts.

10. Discuss new or challenging vocabulary.

11. Provide each student or ask them to provide themselves with colored pencils, markers or crayons, corresponding with the colors assigned to the 4 life areas, e.g., Leisure = blue, Individual care = green, Free/unscheduled time = red, Efforts in school/work activities = yellow.

12. Instruct students to color each section of their balance wheel with one of the 4 colors, depending on how they spend that hour of the day. All 24 hours will be colored in. The use of color will be a visual demonstration of balance/imbalance.

13. Share responses as a class and assist students in analyzing their balance wheels for areas of difficulty.

14. Distribute a second copy of the handout as a follow-up activity for making needed changes in their daily schedules.

15. Process benefits of this activity.

16. Close with a brief summary of the activity and new concepts that were learned.

B. 1. Distribute handouts. Discuss concept of life balance and relationship to one's own stress level and self-concept.

2. Encourage students to complete the handout by writing in all of their specific daily activities, e.g., completing homework, studying for tests, bathing, exercising, talking on the phone, eating, sleeping.

3. Ask students to categorize these activities into life areas: leisure, individual care, free/unscheduled time, and efforts in school/work activities.

4. Share responses as a class and assist students in analyzing their balance wheels for areas of difficulty.

5. Process benefits of this activity.

6. Close with a summary of the activity and new concepts that were learned.

# PROCRASTINATION

| Things I put off doing | Feelings as a result | Is it really a priority? | Action Plan |
|---|---|---|---|
| | | ☐ Yes  ☐ No | |
| | | ☐ Yes  ☐ No | |
| | | ☐ Yes  ☐ No | |
| | | ☐ Yes  ☐ No | |
| | | ☐ Yes  ☐ No | |

*"Time offers us possibilities to create opportunities."*

PROCRASTINATION

I.  PURPOSE:

To improve time management skills.

II.  GENERAL COMMENTS:

Procrastination is an ineffective way of managing time. By assessing a task's relative priority, one can use an "action plan" to deal with specific procrastinations.

III.  POSSIBLE ACTIVITIES:

A.  1.  Discuss new or challenging vocabulary.

2.  Distribute handout. Ask the class to explain the illustration and how it relates to the topic being discussed.

3.  Use the following, or one of your own, as an example to illustrate the concept:

| THINGS I PUT OFF DOING | FEELINGS | IS IT A PRIORITY? | ACTION PLAN |
|---|---|---|---|
| homework | guilty unsuccessful | yes | I will do homework every night from 7-8 p.m. |

4.  Ask class to list things that they put off doing in different areas of their lives, e.g., personal, family, school, recreational areas. Brainstorm on chalkboard.

5.  Discuss feelings and priorities for each example. Ask for a volunteer to create an action plan for each example. Recall prior discussion of realistic, achievable goal setting (Unit 6).

6.  Instruct the class to complete the handout, describing something that they put off doing in each area of their lives. If they need assistance, allow them to use the examples from the chalkboard. Encourage them to use examples of their own.

7.  Instruct the class to share their responses, encouraging feedback from others.

8.  Process benefits of positive time management skills.

9.  Close by asking each student to respond with one new idea that they learned from this activity.

B.  1.  Brainstorm with class tasks most often delayed or left undone, and list on chalkboard.

2.  Encourage each student to choose one from the board, other than their own, and give a possible action plan (perhaps one that has been successful for them in the past).

3.  Encourage students to complete handout and facilitate discussion, encouraging feedback from others.

4.  Process benefits of positive time management skills.

5.  Close with the request that each student share one action plan that s/he will begin.

# Let's pretend - a friend

Male ☐ / Female ☐

Approximate age _____

Physical Appearance _____

_____

Personality / Beliefs / Values _____

_____

Other Special Talents / Interests / Abilities _____

_____

---

What would he / she offer you? _____

_____

What would you need from him / her? _____

_____

What would you offer him / her? _____

_____

---

Have you ever had anyone like this in your life? _____

Who? _____

Is there anyone in your life that could be this person? _____

Who? _____

If no, how could you go about finding this friend? _____

_____

# Let's pretend -
# a friend

## I. PURPOSE:

To evaluate qualities and values of friends and friendships.

## II. GENERAL COMMENTS:

Friendships are an important aspect of many people's lives. Recognizing the values one has regarding friends/friendship might enhance a more active approach to these relationships.

## III. POSSIBLE ACTIVITIES:

A. 1. Discuss new or challenging vocabulary.

2. Brainstorm with class examples of each category in the two upper boxes, and list on chalkboard, e.g., Physical appearance — brown hair, tall, blue eyes, well-dressed.

3. Instruct class to complete their handout, referring to the chalkboard if necessary.

4. Encourage students to complete bottom box individually.

5. Facilitate discussion of responses.

6. Process benefits of activity.

7. To close, instruct the class to circle each characteristic listed on their handout that they recognize in themselves.

8. Inquire why they think they were instructed to circle their own characteristics, and how this relates to evaluating potential friends/friendships.

B. 1. Discuss role of friends/friendships in people's lives.

2. Instruct students to complete handout.

3. Collect handouts and read aloud one at a time, encouraging students to guess the author of each.

4. Summarize as a class what action each will take as a result of this activity.

# What DO I Value ?

Our sense of well-being can be greatly enhanced by participating in activities we value. When we avoid or are prevented from participating, inner conflict can result.

**Directions:** Column [A] List your 5 most valued activities.

[B] Note what activities you participate in to express these values.

[C] Note what prevents you from participating or why you avoid this activity.

| I value: [A] | I participate in this by: [B] | I am prevented from or avoid participating in this by: [C] |
|---|---|---|
| Loyalty | Keeping secrets. Defending my friends. | Gossiping. Not being there when my friends need me. |
| Music | I listen to tapes while walking or exercising. | Watching TV every evening after school / work instead of listening to my tapes. |
| 1. | | |
| 2. | | |
| 3. | | |
| 4. | | |
| 5. | | |

# What DO I Value ?

I.  PURPOSE:

   To promote values clarification by evaluating one's five highest values.

II.  GENERAL COMMENTS:

   Clarifying values allows one to know himself/herself better. Decisions can be influenced with developed insight and possible changes can therefore occur.

III.  POSSIBLE ACTIVITIES:

   A.  1. Discuss new or challenging vocabulary.

      2. Discuss values clarification by presenting handout using description and examples provided.

      3. Write the following categories on the chalkboard:
         REQUIRES MONEY
         CAN BE ENJOYED ALONE
         CAN BE ENJOYED WITH OTHER PEOPLE
         NEEDS PLANNING
         SEASONAL ACTIVITY
         DIFFERENT FROM ANYONE IN THE CLASS
         NEEDS SPECIAL EQUIPMENT/TRAINING
         (any of your own)

      4. Instruct the class to choose 5 categories and to write one in each box.

      5. Instruct the class to write one thing/activity they value in each category, e.g.,
         REQUIRES MONEY — movies, concerts.
         CAN BE ENJOYED ALONE — crafts, model-building.
         CAN BE ENJOYED WITH OTHER PEOPLE — team sports.
         NEEDS PLANNING — travel, vacations.
         SEASONAL ACTIVITY — sunbathing, downhill skiing.
         DIFFERENT FROM ANYONE IN THE CLASS — silversmithing, rock-collecting.
         SPECIAL EQUIPMENT/TRAINING — cross-country skiing, gymnastics.

      6. Encourage class to complete handout.

      7. Ask each student to present most interesting example.

      8. An alternative is to collect, read aloud, and ask class to guess the author of each.

      9. Process benefit of this activity.

      10. Close by asking each student to select one activity that s/he was reminded of or became interested in during the activity, and set a goal to participate in it again before next SEALS session.

   B.  1. Discuss values clarification and present handout, using description and examples provided at top of page.

      2. Encourage students to complete handout.

      3. Instruct students to select their most interesting, unusual, or favorite activity.

      4. Ask for a volunteer to play "20 Questions". The volunteer stands in front of the room. The class is instructed to guess the activity by asking no more than 20 questions which can only be answered with a "yes" or "no" response, e.g.,
         "Is it an activity that can be enjoyed alone?"
         "Is it reading?" etc.
         List each question on chalkboard. If the class has not guessed the identity of the activity, then the volunteer must reveal it.

      5. Class can be divided into 2 teams competing against each other. The team who asked the least amount of questions to discover the identity of the activity is the winner.

      6. Process benefits of the activity.

      7. Close by asking each student to identify one activity s/he was either reminded of or learned about during the class, and to set a goal to participate in that activity before the next SEALS session.

# My motto
## that I live by...

# My motto
## that I hope to live by...

# My motto that I live by...

## I. PURPOSE:

To promote a positive self-image by identifying mottos one lives by and hopes to live by.

## II. GENERAL COMMENTS:

A motto is a brief sentence or phrase used to state what one believes in. A motto that one values can be a powerful way to strengthen self-identity and improve self-image.

## III. POSSIBLE ACTIVITIES:

A. 1. Define "motto" and brainstorm several mottos on chalkboard. Refer to the "MOTTO GAME", page 21, for a list of possible mottos.

   2. Distribute handouts and instruct students to write, draw or symbolize a motto they live by and hope to live by (without allowing other students to see their papers). Students' names should not be written on handout.
   Example:
   a. all for one and one for all.       b. one day at a time.

   3. Post each student's handout around room in "gallery fashion".

   4. Allow 5 minutes for students to browse.

   5. Encourage students to guess which motto belongs to each student, one-by-one, and then allow time for the originator to describe and discuss his/her thoughts.

   6. Process benefits of identifying mottos.

   7. Close with students creating a class motto.

B. 1. Discuss definition of motto, its impact on life-choices and decisions, and ultimately its effect on self-image.

   2. Instruct all students to write 3 mottos on separate strips of paper, and place in basket.

   3. Taking turns, pass the basket so that all students take one strip of paper. Instruct each student to read the motto aloud, explain what it means to them, and possible influences on one's way of life.

   4. Encourage all students who live by these mottos to share their insights.

   5. Distribute handouts and instruct class to write, draw or symbolize a motto they live by, and hope to live by. This can be done as a follow-up activity if time does not permit.

   6. Process benefits of identifying mottos.

   7. Close with students creating a class motto.

## WHAT MOTIVATES ME?

Rank:   #1 = most motivating to #12 = least motivating

_____ enjoyment/fun

_____ family and/or friendships

_____ independence/freedom

_____ possessions

_____ mental health

_____ money/savings

_____ personal achievements

_____ physical health/fitness

_____ power/authority/strength

_____ school achievements

_____ security/safety

_____ popularity/status


Who can you tell that your #1 is a high-ranking motivator? _____

What benefit might you derive? _____


Who can you tell that your #2 is a high-ranking motivator? _____

What benefit might you derive? _____


Who can you tell that your #11 is a low-ranking motivator? _____

What benefit might you derive? _____


Who can you tell that your #12 is a low-ranking motivator? _____

What benefit might you derive? _____

I. PURPOSE:

To develop an understanding of one's personal motivation by ranking the 12 motivators listed.

To recognize with which significant people this information might be shared to increase performance and satisfaction.

II. GENERAL COMMENTS:

Knowing what our motivators are and being able to express them, may increase performance and satisfaction. (As teachers, it is important to know what motivates our students so that we can better plan our curriculum and daily lesson plans.)

III. POSSIBLE ACTIVITIES:

A. 1. Discuss new or challenging vocabulary.

2. Prepare enough slips of paper for each member of the class to receive one.

3. Instruct students to write 1 motivator on each and put in a "hat".

4. Encourage students to select one and describe the importance of their motivator to the class.

5. Distribute handouts and instruct class to complete as indicated.

6. Process importance of identifying motivators.

7. Close by asking each student to identify their #1 motivator.

B. 1. Instruct class to complete the handout individually.

2. Encourage students to create, on the back of the handout, a magazine picture collage, separated into two sections. On the right-hand side of the paper, place words, pictures, and/or symbols representing high motivators. On the left-hand side, represent low motivators. If magazines are not available, the students can draw or list their motivators.

3. Facilitate discussion of personal motivators by asking the following questions:

a. What do the "pictures" represent?

b. Why did you place them on that side of the paper?

c. What people in your life know that these are high or low motivators?

4. Process importance of this information.

5. Close by asking class to identify one member of the class who had the same high motivators. Instruct them to pair up, discuss their mutual interests, and create an action plan to enjoy the same high motivator together, recalling prior discussions of realistic, achievable goal setting.

6. Instruct them to share their action plan with the class, encouraging feedback and positive affirmations for their action plan.

# LEISURE VALUES

| Leisure Activity | Alone | With Others | Inside | Outside | Active | Passive | Challenging | Risky | Relaxing | Funny | Serious | Thought-Provoking | Competitive | Offers Distractions | Self-Development | Cultural | Creative | Helpful to Others | Other |
|---|---|---|---|---|---|---|---|---|---|---|---|---|---|---|---|---|---|---|---|
| | | | | | | | | | | | | | | | | | | | |
| | | | | | | | | | | | | | | | | | | | |
| | | | | | | | | | | | | | | | | | | | |
| | | | | | | | | | | | | | | | | | | | |
| | | | | | | | | | | | | | | | | | | | |
| | | | | | | | | | | | | | | | | | | | |

Describe the differences between the leisure activities that you NOW do and the activities which you would MOST LIKE to or would prefer to do?

_____

_____

_____

_____

_____

_____

What is one new leisure activity you will get involved in that reflects some of these values?

_____

# LEISURE VALUES

## I. PURPOSE:

To identify values regarding leisure by analyzing qualities of activities.

To identify present leisure habits and compare them to leisure values.

## II. GENERAL COMMENTS:

It is important to be aware of the reasons certain leisure activities are enjoyed, so that efforts can be made to continue having satisfying experiences. Oftentimes, people say that they value certain types of activities, yet, do not engage in these. Leisure habits may be modified, if needed, to include values and increase satisfaction.

## III. POSSIBLE ACTIVITIES:

A. 1. Discuss new or challenging vocabulary.

2. Explain concept of balancing work, leisure and self-care activities.
(See page 69-BALANCE YOUR LIFE)

3. Make an overhead transparency of the handout, projecting the handout so that the entire class can view. List one activity in the first box as an example. Check all qualities that have "attracted" or interested you in this activity.

4. Distribute handouts. Instruct the class to complete handout by identifying 6 leisure activities they enjoy, past and present.

5. Next, ask the class to check all qualities that "attract" them to or interest them in each of these activities.

6. Encourage them to write a paragraph describing the differences/similarities between their leisure habits and their leisure values, and answer remaining questions on handout.

7. Facilitate discussion regarding insights, and process benefits of leisure involvement.

8. Close by listing their responses to the last question.

B. 1. Write each of the 18 listed leisure qualities on separate index cards and shuffle.

2. Instruct students to take turns choosing a card and identifying one leisure activity they enjoy which has that quality. Continue until all 18 are discussed and/or every student has had a chance to participate.

3. Distribute handout and instruct class to complete.

4. Facilitate discussion regarding insights, and process benefits of leisure involvement.

5. Close with discussion of their responses to the last question.

# TEACHERS' BONUS SECTION

■ To be used if SEALS+PLUS will be offered as an individualized program.
(*See Questions and Suggested Responses, page h, for further explanation.*)

# SAMPLE
# NEWS RELEASE

— ATTENTION: PARENTS —
Self-Esteem And Life Skills classes
for students are available now!

SCHOOL: _____

PHONE: _____

SCHOOL ADDRESS: _____

IF YOUR CHILD COULD BENEFIT BY SELF-AWARENESS IN. . .
ASSERTIVENESS, ANGER MANAGEMENT,
APPROPRIATE RISK TAKING, EMOTION IDENTIFICATION OR
PROBLEM SOLVING, CONSIDER:

**S**ELF
**E**STEEM
**A**ND
**L**IFE
**S**KILLS

## AN ACTIVE PROCESS OF LEARNING NEW SKILLS

FACULTY PARTICIPANTS:    MR. DYLAN – ROOM 1        MRS. ALLEN – ROOM 12
                         MISS WOODLAND – ROOM 3    MR. WILHELM – ROOM 18
                         MRS. BAKER – ROOM 5       MISS FRENCH – ROOM 201

PLEASE SIGN AND RETURN TO THE GUIDANCE OFFICE A.S.A.P.
CHECK ONE:

_____ Call or send me more information.

_____ I give my permission for my child, _____, to participate in the
SEALS+PLUS program.

X _____    DATE _____
*(Parent/Guardian Signature)*

# QUESTIONS AND SUGGESTED RESPONSES

The **SEALS+PLUS book** *can be implemented in school settings in a variety of ways. Specific handouts or units can be chosen by the teachers to complement existing programs within a regular or specialized curriculum, or SEALS+PLUS can be developed as a special class where students meet to focus on* **S***elf-***E***steem* **A***nd* **L***ife* **S***kills topics. The following is designed for the latter:*

## What is the SEALS+PLUS program?
A program designed to educate children and adolescents in self-esteem and life skills which include assertiveness, anger management, appropriate risk taking, problem solving, and emotion identification.

## Who is teaching this class?
Certified teachers and concerned staff members.

## Do the teachers have special training?
Most classes will be facilitated by college graduates, many with graduate degrees in education or counseling. (If special training is desired, it is available through Wellness Reproductions Inc. - 800/669-9208).

## Are there any additional fees, supplies, or costs required?
They may be required to furnish art supplies, such as markers, pencils, or crayons, upon occasion.

## May I (the parent/guardian) participate or observe?
Although your participation would be valuable, it is not recommended. A copy of the handouts and activities can be made available to you upon your request.

## How are the participants chosen?
There are several ways: by grades, by the parent's, teacher's or guidance office's referral, or by the student's own request.

## Will the class discussions be private and confidential?
Every effort will be made to ensure confidentiality.

## How long is each session?
Each session is presented in one regular class period.

## How long is the program?
Answers will vary depending on students' needs, time availability, and school budget.

## What are the topics?
There are 15 in all; anger management, assertion, communication skills, coping skills, emotion identification, goal setting, health awareness, money management, problem-solving, risk taking, self-esteem, stress management, support systems, time management, and values clarification.

## Will my child's grades be affected?
As self-esteem and life skills improve, so will academic performance. If your child is excused from a class in order to participate in the SEALS+PLUS program, and chooses not to make up the missed or incomplete work, then there is a possibility that his/her grades may reflect that decision.

## Can my child begin/leave the program at any time?
If the SEALS+PLUS program is to be conducted outside of the regular content area curriculum, your child can start at anytime that there is a new SEALS+PLUS program beginning. Even though it is not preferred, s/he can also participate once the program has begun, but only with consent of the teacher and the class. Your child can leave the program, upon your request at any time.

## Why must I sign an authorization?
Your child might not be in his/her regularly scheduled class. Anytime there is a deviation from his/her schedule, it must be with the permission of the parents/guardians.

## Has this program been approved by the school board?
Answers will vary according to your school policy.

# SAMPLE LETTER TO PARENTS/GUARDIANS

LETTERHEAD of YOUR SCHOOL

ADDRESS
CITY, STATE, ZIP
(000) 000-0000

Dear Parent/Guardian,

Your child, _____, has been invited to participate in a self-esteem group. The group will meet once a week for a nine week period.

The goal of this group is to generate a sense of belonging, support, acceptance, and assistance. Also, the group will provide a social setting in which to promote self-esteem, learning, and development of interpersonal skills.

If you have further questions, please call the guidance office at 000-0000.

Sincerely,


*(Signature of Teacher/Facilitator)*


Parent's Signature _____

Please return to Teacher/Facilitator.

— C —

# LETTER TO CLASSROOM TEACHERS

TO:_____  H.R.:_____  DATE:_____
     *(Teacher/Facilitator)*

Dear Mr./Ms./Mrs._____,
   Your student, _____, will be participating in the
SEALS+PLUS program.  SEALS stands for Self-Esteem And Life Skills.  The class will meet
once a week for a _____ week period, beginning on _____ and
concluding on _____.
   The goal of this class is to generate a sense of belonging, support, acceptance, and
assistance.  Also, the class will provide a social setting in which to promote self-esteem,
learning, and development of interpersonal skills.
   Please excuse _____ from your _____
(period/class) each week on _____(day).  S/he is of the understanding that
s/he is responsible for all incomplete or missed work.  Please sign the attached
permission slip and return it to me as soon as possible.
   If you have any further questions, please feel free to see me in Room _____.
   Your assistance and cooperation are greatly appreciated.

Sincerely,

X _____
   *(Teacher/Facilitator's Signature)*

_____

TO:_____
     *(Teacher/Facilitator)*
RE: SEALS

I have spoken with _____ regarding his/her participation in the
                        *(Student's Name)*
SEALS+PLUS program.  I believe s/he would benefit from this program and give my
consent to excuse him/her from class contingent on his/her intent to complete all missed
work.  I reserve the right to request his/her participation in regular classroom activities if
the need arises.

X _____  Date_____
   *(Classroom Teacher's Signature)*

Comments: _____

_____

_____

– d –

# PRE-SEALS+PLUS INTERVIEW PROTOCOL

Name of Student_____     H.R.: _____

Teacher/Facilitator_____

Date: _____     Group: _____

SEND NOTE / PERMISSION SLIP / HALL PASS /
REQUESTING INTERVIEW                                          _____

WELCOME STUDENT                                              _____

DESCRIBE PURPOSE OF SEALS PROGRAM                            _____

DISCUSS SELECTION PROCESS                                    _____

DISCUSS TOPICS TO BE COVERED                                 _____

DISCUSS EXPECTED OUTCOME/RESULTS                             _____

ADDRESS STUDENT'S CONCERNS                                   _____

OBTAIN COPY OF STUDENT'S CLASS SCHEDULE                      _____

OBTAIN PERMISSION SLIP FROM PARENTS / GUARDIANS              _____

SEND LETTER TO CLASSROOM TEACHER                             _____

GIVE SELF-ESTEEM PRE-TEST                                    _____

Concerns: _____

Recommendations: _____

Comments: _____

X _____
　　(Student's Signature)

X _____
　　(Teacher/Counselor/Facilitator's Signature)

# STUDENT PRE/POST SELF-EVALUATION

NAME: _____

GROUP: _____ DATE: _____

RATE YOURSELF (✔) IN THE FOLLOWING AREAS:

|  | POOR | FAIR | GOOD | EXCELLENT |
|---|---|---|---|---|
| 1. Anger Management |  |  |  |  |
| 2. Assertiveness |  |  |  |  |
| 3. Communication Skills |  |  |  |  |
| 4. Coping Skills |  |  |  |  |
| 5. Emotion Identification |  |  |  |  |
| 6. Goal Setting/Achieving |  |  |  |  |
| 7. Physical Fitness |  |  |  |  |
| 8. Money Management |  |  |  |  |
| 9. Problem Solving |  |  |  |  |
| 10. Risk Taking |  |  |  |  |
| 11. Self-Esteem |  |  |  |  |
| 12. Stress Management |  |  |  |  |
| 13. Support Systems |  |  |  |  |
| 14. Time Management |  |  |  |  |
| 15. Values Clarification |  |  |  |  |
| 16. Personal Appearance |  |  |  |  |
| 17. Punctuality |  |  |  |  |
| 18. Grades/Achievement |  |  |  |  |
| 19. Relationships |  |  |  |  |
| 20. Conduct/Behavior |  |  |  |  |
| TOTALS = |  |  |  |  |

– f –

# GROUP RULES

1. CONFIDENTIALITY

2. _____

3. _____

4. _____

5. _____

6. _____

7. _____

# GROUP FORMAT

**INTRODUCTION** (5-10 minutes)
1. Present, define, and discuss new or challenging vocabulary.
2. Present topic through demonstration or discussion of illustrations.
3. Outline and discuss session goals.
4. Give directions for activity with clarification as needed.

**APPLICATION** (20-30 minutes)
1. Implement age-appropriate activity:
   a.) Activity A is focused at middle school level.
   b.) Activity B is focused at high school level.
2. Note class interaction throughout.

**CONCLUSION** (5-10 minutes)
1. Discussion period (processing).
   Connect the activity to the goals by asking:
   "Can someone sum up today's activity?"
   "Why did we do this?"
   "What did you get out of this?"
2. Closure
   a.) Brief summary by teacher or students.
   b.) Reminder of next class/session.

# Supplemental Role-Plays

While arguing on the telephone with
a close friend, s/he becomes
angry and hangs up on you.
What would you do?

Your teacher gave you a lower grade
on a report than you feel you deserved.
One way to approach this situation would be . . .

Friends begin to sing
"Happy Birthday" to you in a public place.
How do you react to this
embarrassing situation?

While talking with a friend, you remembered
that s/he borrowed money from you two weeks
ago with a promise to repay it the next day.
S/he has not paid you back yet.
What's your next move?

You see someone cheating on a test.
A. It's someone you like.
B. It's someone you dislike.
What would you do in each case?

A friend invites you to a party
and you really don't want to go.
What do you say or do?

You are asked by a friend to give some
additional help in a crisis situation. You
feel that you have already done your share.
How would you respond?

A casual friend or teacher constantly
teases you in a joking way.
This is really beginning to annoy you.
What do you do?

You have made plans with two friends.
While you are getting ready, another friend
unexpectedly arrives and asks if s/he can come
along. You don't want to include him/her.
What can you say?

You are in charge of a group project for a
social studies class that is due next week. All but
one student have worked hard on the project.
What do you say to him/her?

A friend/relative gives you a gift
that you really don't like or want.
What's your response?

A very close friend constantly
interrupts you while you are speaking.
How can you handle this?

You see someone that you
would really like to meet.
How could you go about it?

A friend of yours shows you a new outfit
that was just purchased for a very special
occasion, and asks for your opinion.
You think it's in very poor taste.
What do you say?

You are in study hall and really need to
concentrate on a difficult math assignment.
The students next to you are talking
loudly and cracking chewing gum.
You respond by . . .

You are out with a friend for dinner at a
fast food restaurant. The last 2 times, you paid
the bill. Your friend places his/her order
and then says, "By the way, I'm a little short
on cash, could you help me out?"
What's your response?

# Supplemental Role-Plays

Your friend used to call and spend time with you often, but has not lately, and for no apparent reason. You feel very close to this person and would like to know where you stand with him/her. What would you do?

You are having trouble writing a paper for English class and don't quite understand the assignment. How would you ask for help?

---

Your best friend tells you that you should lose weight. Your response is . . .

You arrive home from school and find that your mother has volunteered your time to help out a neighbor. You have other plans. You say . . .

---

Your best friend gives you the "silent treatment", instead of saying what's on his/her mind. You say . . .

A friend, teacher, schoolmate, fellow employee, or supervisor continuously tells racial or ethnic jokes. You feel uncomfortable. What do you do?

---

You'd like an increase in allowance/salary. You say . . .

You have been invited to a friend's house for dinner. When dinner is served, it is something you are allergic to. What do you do?

---

You've been talking on the phone for awhile with a friend. You would like to end the conversation. What would you say?

Your girlfriend/boyfriend always compares you to her/his last boyfriend/girlfriend. More often than not, it is not in a favorable way. What do you do?

---

You are in a sporting goods store and the salesperson is pressuring you to purchase a very expensive item. Your response is . . .

You have been trying to use the phone all evening, but your younger sister/brother has been monopolizing it. Your phonecall is important. What do you do or say?

---

You have been bothered several times this past week by a caller who has repeatedly tried to sell you magazines. The caller contacts you again with the same magazine proposition. When you answer the phone this time, you say . . .

You have just finished cleaning the bathroom and are proud of the job that you've done. When you return later, you observe that other family members have trashed it. What's your response?

---

An acquaintance has asked to borrow something of yours that is very important to you. What do you say or do?

Your best friend is planning on running away. S/he is trying to persuade you into going along. You don't want to go, nor do you want him/her to go. What do you say or do?

# GLOSSARY

**affirmations PAGE: 52**
self-esteem boosters; ways to make us fully conscious and aware of the daily choices we make; positive powerful self-statements concerning the ways in which we desire to think, feel, and behave

**aggression PAGE: 1**
behavior which violates the rights of others; often humiliates, dominates, or puts the other person down, rather than expressing one's honest emotions or feelings

**aggressive PAGE: 7 & 8**
communication style which evidences hostile and/or extreme behavior

**alternatives PAGE: 20**
options/choices you have when faced with a problem

**anger management PAGE: 1**
the most effective and assertive style of coping with anger situations; steps include recognizing emotions, events and circumstances, considering options, choosing, communicating openly

**assertive PAGE: 7 & 8**
a learned communication style that is honest and direct; a way of communicating with others in a more satisfying way without sacrificing personal needs and/or self-respect, and without violating or infringing upon the rights of others

**assumption PAGE: 9**
a fact or statement that is taken for granted or supposed to be true

**black and white thinking PAGE: 4 & 22**
refers to absolutes or all-or-nothing statements; disallows compromise

**blaming PAGE: 25**
a way of giving up control by not recognizing or owning one's own feelings

**body language PAGE: 17**
a component of communication in which a message is transmitted nonverbally using eye contact, body posture, gestures, facial expressions, and personal space

**boosters PAGE: 55**
actions/thoughts/ways that enhance self-esteem

**boundaries PAGE: 19**
indicators of an extent or limit

**brain overload PAGE: 65**
an overwhelming feeling that occurs when there are an increasing number of pressures and responsibilities to be addressed

**brainstorming PAGE: 44**
a problem-solving activity that involves the spontaneous contributions of ideas

**busters PAGE: 55**
actions/thoughts/ways that lower self-esteem

**challenges PAGE: 45**
a demanding task that calls for special effort or dedication

**community resources PAGE: 64**
agencies/facilities/organizations that offer services within the community

**coping skills PAGE: 42**
a behavior that allows one to deal with or attempt to overcome problems, challenges, stressors, and difficult situations

**decision making PAGE: 45**
making up one's mind by considering options and making a choice

**diary PAGE: 6 & 10**
a journal for self-awareness, self-disclosure, and/or creativity where current experiences, actions, behaviors, thoughts, feelings, observations, reflections, and responses are recorded at regular intervals for personal use

**efforts in school/work activities PAGE: 69**
one of the four components of a balanced daily schedule involving employment, along with responsibilities in and around school, home, church, clubs, groups, and organizations

**escalating PAGE: 3**
a heated and extreme reaction to a situation where recognition and acceptance of an emotion is bypassed resulting in rage; expression is hostile and aggressive

**free/unscheduled time PAGE: 69**
one of four components of a balanced daily schedule, comprised of time allotted for relaxation and "down-time"

**goals PAGE: 29**
an aim, an objective, or intention; can be short-term, long-term, or very long-term

**"I" statements PAGE: 25**
effective, honest and open way to powerfully assert yourself; takes responsibility for own feelings, thoughts and actions

**imprint PAGE: 51**
a lasting impression, effect, or influence

**individual care PAGE: 69**
one of four components of a balanced daily schedule, involving rest, sleep, nutrition, exercise, hygiene, grooming, medical care, self-management, and relationships

**learned behaviors PAGE: 2**
skills, thoughts, actions, or tendencies acquired through observations, experiences, and/or practices

**leisure PAGE: 40**
free time from work or responsibilities; a time for nurturance through activities that are completed without rush or haste

# GLOSSARY

**lifesavers PAGE: 62**
support systems which are vital in effective stress management

**limits PAGE: 19**
boundaries; setting a point which cannot or must not be passed without causing stress or invasion of rights or personal space

**long-term PAGE: 29**
usually used to describe goals/objectives which are accomplished after an extended period of time

**measurable PAGE: 29**
a criteria, basis, or standard; an estimate or appraisal; having an observable limit or amount

**mobilize PAGE: 5**
to shift into action

**motivators PAGE: 74**
forces or influences which give incentive or drive

**motto PAGE: 21 & 73**
a saying adopted as a principle of behavior

**passive PAGE: 7 & 8**
communication style which allows rights and feelings to be violated, resulting in a loss of self-respect

**personal power PAGE: 25**
influence, control, authority over one's self, the ability to act assertively; a recognized capacity for performance

**priority PAGE: 70**
something that requires immediate attention

**procrastinate PAGE: 70**
to intentionally and habitually put off doing something that needs to be done

**realistic PAGE: 29**
practical, accurate, achievable

**reframe PAGE: 15**
to adjust and re-express self-defeating statements which will increase personal strength and self-control

**regimen PAGE: 35**
a plan, a system designed to improve health

**risks PAGE: 45**
a possibility or chance resulting in gains and/or losses

**roadblocks PAGE: 20**
something that blocks progress or prevents accomplishment of goals

**self-defeating PAGE: 15**
acting in ways which prevent personal progress

**self-disclosure PAGE: 14**
sharing or revealing personal information held close or of a private nature

**self-talk PAGE: 15**
thoughts one has or statements one makes about oneself, which may be positive or negative, and directly influence the level of one's self-esteem

**self-esteem PAGE: 19**
valuing oneself; a confidence and satisfaction in oneself; self-respect

**sense of loss PAGE: 27**
a definite, but often vague, awareness associated with grief

**serenity PAGE: 23**
calm; peacefulness; quietness of spirit

**short-term PAGE: 29**
term often used to describe goals/objectives which can be achieved in a short period of time

**sibling PAGE: 13**
a brother or sister irrespective of age

**stressors PAGE: 61**
stimuli that cause tension

**stuffing PAGE: 2**
an ineffective coping skill in anger management usually associated with a passive style of communication; characterized by behaviors that prevent open, honest, and direct communication

**supports PAGE: 63**
someone/thing that offers assistance or comfort, and advocates healthy behavior

**symptom PAGE: 1 & 6**
a sign or indication of a problem

**task PAGE: 30**
usually an assignment/activity that must be finished within a certain time limit

**triggers PAGE: 6**
stimuli which initiate a strong reaction or response

**value PAGE: 72**
to give worth, usefulness, importance; to hold in high esteem, consider or rate highly

**very long-term PAGE: 29**
term that describes a goal/objective that can be accomplished over a very extensive period of time as a result of achieving a series of short-term goals/objectives

**well-being PAGE: 72**
the state of being healthy emotionally, physically, socially, spiritually, etc.

# FACILITATOR SESSION EVALUATION FORM

A. Topic: _____

   Date: _____

B. Goals: _____

   _____

   Were the goals accomplished? _____

C. How effective was your introduction? _____

   If you were to lead a similar session again, what changes might you make? _____

   _____

D. How effective was your application of the activity?_____

   If you were to lead a similar session again, what changes might you make? _____

   _____

E. How effective was your conclusion of this session? _____

   If you were to lead a similar session again, what changes might you make? _____

   _____

F. Were you adequately prepared for the session? _____

   _____

   _____

G. How did you function as a teacher/facilitator/group leader?_____

   _____

   Were you effective? _____

H. Was the class interaction/response as you anticipated? _____

   If it wasn't, what can you attribute this to? _____

   _____

   _____

I. In the future, what might you do differently as a teacher/leader/facilitator? _____

   _____

   _____

# EXIT INTERVIEW PROTOCOL

STUDENT: _____ DATE: _____

TEACHER/FACILITATOR: _____ CLASS: _____


Discuss goals of SEALS+PLUS.  Were goals met? _____

Were student's personal expectations of the program met? _____

Were new skills presented/learned? _____

List new skills: _____

Were topics relevant/meaningful/helpful/age-appropriate? _____

Was information useful? _____

Were the skills presented realistic? _____

Did the class activities help to integrate the concepts being taught? _____

Was enough time scheduled for activities? _____

Favorite topic/activity?  List reasons why. _____

Least favorite topic/activity?  List reasons why. _____

Comparing results of Student Pre/Post Self-Evaluation:

    how has SEALS+PLUS helped? _____

    how has SEALS+PLUS hindered? _____

    how can SEALS+PLUS be improved? _____

Present and/or discuss:

    CERTIFICATE (page 54) or _____

    AFFIRMATIONS ... A+ ME (page 52) or _____

    COMMUNITY RESOURCES (page 64). _____


X _____ (Student)


X _____ (Teacher)


_____ (Date)

# STUDENT EVALUATION

1 - STRONGLY AGREE    2 - AGREE    3 - NO OPINION    4 - DISAGREE    5 - STRONGLY DISAGREE

Goals of SEALS+PLUS program were adequately presented.    _____

New vocabulary was discussed and explained.    _____

Topics were relevant and useful.    _____

Activities were appropriate for age and grade level.    _____

Teacher/facilitator was well-prepared.    _____

Confidentiality was respected.    _____

Established group rules were followed.    _____

Goals of SEALS+PLUS were accomplished.    _____

Students interacted well with one another.    _____

Improvements in self-esteem and life skills have been
    observed by self.    _____

Improvements in self-esteem and life skills have been
    observed by others.    _____

SEALS+PLUS program would benefit other students and
    should continue in our school.    _____


SUGGESTIONS/COMMENTS:_____

_____

_____

_____

— O —

# FEEDBACK SEALS+PLUS

Please photocopy, complete, and mail to
Wellness Reproductions Inc., 23945 Mercantile Road, Beachwood, Ohio 44122-5924

Check the topics that were of special interest in SEALS+PLUS:

☐ Anger Management     ☐ Assertion     ☐ Communication Skills

☐ Coping Skills     ☐ Emotion Identification

☐ Goal Setting     ☐ Health Awareness     ☐ Money Management

☐ Problem Solving     ☐ Risk Taking

☐ Self-Esteem/Awareness     ☐ Stress Management     ☐ Support Systems

☐ Time Management     ☐ Values Clarification

Comments on SEALS+PLUS: _____

_____

_____

Can this comment be published as an attestation?_____

_____
(*Signature*)

Name _____  Title _____

School _____  Occupation _____

Address _____  Home Address _____

City _____  City _____

State _____  State _____

Phone (work) _____  Phone (home)_____

*(Please fold on dotted lines on reverse side, staple, stamp and mail)*

WELLNESS REPRODUCTIONS INC.
23945 MERCANTILE ROAD
BEACHWOOD, OH 44122-5924